MW01166301

After the Last Heartbeat

After the Last Heartbeat

TOM SCARINCI

as told to Will Norton, Jr.

CHRISTIAN HERALD BOOKS
Chappaqua, New York

Library of Congress Cataloging in Publication Data

Scarinci , Tom.
    After the last heartbeat.

    1. Spinal cord—Surgery—Complications and sequelae—Biography. 2. Anesthesia—Complications and sequelae—Biography. 3. Heart failure—Patiens—Biography. 4. Scarinci, Tom. 5. Christian life—1960- I. Norton, Will. II. Title.
RD594.3.S29 617'.48201'0926 [B] 79-55679
ISBN 0-915684-55-1

Christian Herald, independent, evangelical and interdenominational, is dedicated to publishing wholesome, inspirational and religious books for Christian families. ''The books you can trust.''

First Edition
CHRISTIAN HERALD BOOKS, 40 Overlook Drive, Chappaqua, New York 10514
Printed in the United States of America

MEMBER OF
EVANGELICAL CHRISTIAN
PUBLISHERS ASSOCIATION

Contents

1

We've Lost Him!

A thin orderly wearing hospital green helped Tom Scarinci painfully slide his 235 pound torso onto a cart.

Tom laid his head back and heard the click as the side of the cart was raised into place. He felt the cart start to move as it rolled quietly into the hallway, and he heard the belabored coughing of a patient and the occasional "stat, stat, stat" emergency call for doctors. He noticed the ceiling lights flashing by as he rolled swiftly along the corridor. But his thoughts were elsewhere—on his two-year-old son, Heath, and his beautiful wife, Cheryl. It was they who had given him strength to endure, even through moments when he had contemplated suicide.

Tom reflected on the times when he used to lie flat on the floor while muscle spasms wrenched his once-powerful torso. The nearness of his son provided comfort during those excruciating hours, and he could almost feel Heath's soft, brown curls, the son's head cradled contentedly in the crook of his dad's arm. He remembered the leg-numbing pain that punctuated leisurely Sunday drives through the sun-drenched Santa Cruz Mountains while Cheryl, her blue eyes dancing with excitement, chattered happily about their plans for a new house. And he saw again her brave smile when she waved good-bye to him, brushed quickly at an unwanted tear, and, with head bent, turned toward the house as he backed out of the driveway on his way to the hospital.

She had begged him not to undergo surgery and take the risk of permanent paralysis, but life without the surgery had been sheer misery, a desperate search for relief from his torture. He had given himself so many prescribed injections of Demerol and so many pain-killing pills that he had already been labeled a "drug addict" by some in the medical profession.

He also had serious spiritual problems. Although converted to faith in Jesus Christ as a teenager through the ministry of a street evangelist, he had not grown in the faith. For years he had ignored God's call until, with his strength waning from an undiagnosed infection, he yielded his life completely to the Lord. Eventually he found a place of service at Cliffwood Heights Neighborhood Church, where he was richly rewarded in a ministry to young people and in crisis counseling. However, the nerve-jangling pain had hampered his effectiveness, and doctors now told him there was no future without surgery.

Yet Tom Scarinci's mind had rebelled at the thought of more surgery. For months he had wrestled with his fear of the surgeon's knife, but the searing pain had worn down his resistance. Despite the new techniques of modern surgery, his chances were only fifty-fifty for any relief from the agony that had sent him to hospitals thirty-one times in five years. Now he knew that spinal surgery was necessary, and after today he hoped there would be no more pain.

He had been admitted to Stanford University Medical Center in Palo Alto, California, one of the major health-care complexes in the world, a place of healing to which thousands annually make their pilgrimages to experience the miracles of modern medicine. In desperation and pain they come from almost every nation of the world. Like them, Tom had come, even though this renowned institution could provide no guarantee for his recovery. Its surgeons merely described the delicate nature of the operation and cited the probabilities. Surgery might not ease the pain, they said. Moreover, he might be crippled the rest of his life, and he worried about how this would affect his family.

His eyes glistened as he thought of the abrupt sound of his wife's anxious words when she left his room moments before the orderly had come for him. He had felt the terror in her reticence to leave, so he had casually told her to go have lunch with her mother. He wanted her to know he was not afraid.

Now the doors to the operating room swung open, and he was wheeled in. Gowned and masked nurses and doctors appeared like specters out of a mist while he was eased onto the operating table. He heard a few last words from Dr. Murray Walker, the anesthesiologist, and then, blessed sleep.

The surgery began smoothly, the surgeon deftly cutting a small incision in Tom's lower back. Then Dr. Walker noticed that Tom's lips, earlobes, and fingernails were becoming bluish.

"He's getting cyanotic," Dr. Walker said.

Quickly he glanced at a video screen and saw gross irregularities in the heartbeat. Tom's face was pale and turning blue. There was no blood pressure.

"There's no heart action," a doctor yelled.

"Turn him over," Dr. Walker ordered.

Hurriedly, aides stuffed cotton into the incision and turned Tom onto his back. Every second was precious. The irregular heartbeat may not have been noticed for thirty seconds, and because he was so big, it took another twenty seconds to turn him over.

If the heart could not be restarted, mere moments would be left before any chance of recovery would be gone. A surgeon leaped onto the table and began heart massage, rhythmically pounding against Tom's chest. But the color did not improve.

Another surgeon took his place. He was bigger and could deflate Tom's lungs, and color quickly returned to Tom's face, but his heartbeat was irregular.

The minutes seemed like hours. As one surgeon tired, another took his place, keeping the regular rhythm. Tom's color paled. Then it improved. His pupils dilated several times from lack of oxygen to the brain. Each time, the desperate activity of the doctors intensified.

They couldn't stabilize Tom's condition, and the calm, professional atmosphere became chaotic. Shouting and cursing, the doctors frantically tried to restore a regular heartbeat. More doctors were summoned. Emergency equipment was rolled into place. Adrenalin was injected into the heart, and electric shock was administered.

But nothing worked.

The electrocardiogram showed giant, sweeping waves in rapid succession, indication of drastic heart degeneration. Calcium and other drugs were injected, and the doctors determinedly massaged the heart. Then the heartbeat was lost. It had been fifteen minutes since Dr. Walker first noticed Tom's lips turning blue.

Then, suddenly, a faint heartbeat returned. It wasn't regular, but Tom was young and strong, and there was hope. If they could bring back a regular rhythm, they thought, he could recover.

But they lost the heartbeat again. The activity became panic-like, with more shouting and injections. With every resource available to modern medicine, the doctors battled for Tom's life.

Another half hour passed, a total of forty to fifty minutes of wild activity in which there would be a heartbeat, then it would disappear, and then it would be brought back. Finally, a strong, regular heartbeat was restored.

Now the real struggle began. Tom had been without a regular heartbeat for so long that there had been significant loss of oxygen to the brain, making severe brain damage inevitable. The doctors had to move quickly to limit further cell destruction. Doctors were called who had experimented with a procedure that allowed brain cell activity to slow down so that cells could rest and the self-damaging reaction would be kept to a minimum. If the cells remained normally active without proper oxygen, they would be severely damaged. By slowing their activity, doctors would limit the amount of oxygen that would be needed, and a minimum of brain cell damage would occur. They decided that was the only hope and began the treatment. A large dose of thiopental sodium was injected, and Tom's body was placed on a ''cooler'' bed designed to lower body temperature.

Monitoring devices were attached to his head and chest. A catheter was placed in his arm, tubes were forced down his throat to keep his heart beating and his lungs breathing, and space boots were placed on his feet to facilitate the circulation of blood that was essential to supply as much oxygen to the brain as possible while brain activity was slowed.

Now there were no brain waves. After twenty-four hours the thiopental sodium would wear off, the doctors promised. Then, if the brain waves began, Tom would regain consciousness. But recovery was improbable—indeed, only two persons who had lived after twenty-four hours without brain waves had not had severe brain damage.

Clearly, Tom's condition was critical. He had gone for nearly an hour without a regular heartbeat, and most human beings cannot live more than fifteen minutes in such a state, much less regain consciousness.

His cold and motionless body looked like a corpse, and, when pricked with a needle, there was no reflex of pain. There were no signs of life.

Tom Scarinci was as good as dead.

2
Attempted Escape

I'm Tom Scarinci, that body on the "cooling table." Miraculously, I lived through that traumatic experience on the operating table at Stanford. What's more, although I was as good as dead and showed no signs of brain activity for ten days, I suffered no brain damage. The incident made medical history and changed the lives of hundreds of people in the San Francisco area who pleaded with the Lord for me.

When I entered the hospital, I was desperate. I had reached my lowest point physically in thirty-four years of increasingly frequent health problems. Many of these were caused by my carelessness or impulsiveness, and as the years passed, I couldn't seem to shake off misfortune. Yet God was patient with me. Despite my disobedience, irresponsibility, and preoccupation with showing off, He allowed me to do what I wanted until I got in such a predicament that there was no alternative. I turned myself and everything I owned over to the Lord.

For years He had spoken to me, but, like Jonah, I had tried to avoid Him. My attempts to escape were not caused by a rebelliousness that was nurtured within the Protestant evangelical subculture. In fact, I didn't even know what a Protestant Christian was, much less an evangelical. I had no excuses, however.

My rebelliousness was subtle. I seemed to be a faithful church member, but I was merely developing a spirit of self-indulgence within a ritualistic Catholicism. As the years passed, this perspective developed into a full-blown self-centeredness and self-righteousness. Although I had grown up in a traditional Italian family that professed basic commitments to the Roman Catholic Church, my religious experiences within the church had not been consistent. I earnestly was looking for answers and spent hours studying the Bible and biblical commentaries, but I often allowed job openings, easy money, or some other opportunity to have priority over my deep spiritual needs.

Fortunately, my efforts often were not successful, and I repeatedly was reminded of my spiritual needs. Perhaps nothing reminded me more readily of my needs than the fact that I was a misfit in my own family. My father, Michael Scarinci, had immigrated to the United States and met and married my mother, Mary. They had settled into a house on a five-acre plot on Cook Avenue in Scotch Plains, New Jersey, and had raised five children, Joseph, Danny, Noreen, Michael, Jr., and Marie (Cookie), before my twin brother, Albert, and I were born. So Albert and I actually formed a second family for my parents.

Our family lived in a big, old-fashioned, Victorian house. We occupied eleven rooms on one side, and the Farrars lived in the other half. There was a big screened porch on two sides of the house. After going in the front door, one walked through an entryway to a high-ceilinged living room. Also on that floor were a dining room, kitchen, pantry, and bedroom. A large, spiral staircase led to the four rooms on the second floor and three more on the third floor.

Albert and I had a bedroom on the second floor, above the kitchen, and we could sneak out the window and onto the porch and jump to the ground.

My father had his woodworking shop upstairs in the large, gray barn behind the house. Beside the barn was our chicken coop. We raised chickens and grew our own vegetables. The garden plot was behind the barn, and one of our first jobs when we were growing up was to break up a garden with pitchforks.

Mr. Farrar kept grading equipment and several tractors in the barn. He was in the grading business, and when Albert and I became teenagers, he often loaned us a tractor to shovel snow and earn some extra money.

My father was a furniture refinisher, cabinet maker, and upholsterer who had brought a family tradition of fine craftsmanship with him from Italy. He was a burly man, with massive forearms and powerful shoulders, and his short, thick hands could craft the finest furniture. When I was young, I believed he could do anything. He would do the moving of furniture as well as the handcrafting. I can remember the power he exuded in his slow but steady climb up a set of stairs with a heavy bureau on his back. To me, no one expressed immovable strength as he did.

I knew that no one had a father like mine, but he seemed so distant. I never felt that he knew and understood me. I was awed by his presence, and I cowered under his strong discipline. I felt his domination but none of his love. In fact, although I loved him deeply, I thought he disapproved of love. He gave the impression of being someone who could not be hurt, and, as the years passed, he seemed less and less capable of showing any feeling.

Yet until he suffered two strokes, his craftsmanship showed great sensitivity. Moose and deer heads hung on the walls of his cluttered shop, and I have warm boyhood memories of his pushing the wavy black hair from his eyes as he labored intensely on a piece, reworking it into an elegant piece of furniture. His shop was also a place for many of the men in the neighborhood to meet and discuss politics and business. One of those men once put his arm on my shoulder and said, "Tom, if you're ever as good at this business as your dad, you'll be the best."

My father wanted us to be the best. His attitude was that you do the best job possible. He was always trying to prove he was the best, and he seemed to need recognition from everyone but his family. So he would buy other people things his own family could not afford. One time, when Albert and I were in the early grades, he gave five hundred dollars to a friend, and as a result, we were not able to buy school clothes.

My family's standards were high. My father didn't like a liar. He was an honest man, and he expected his son to be honest. One day I played hooky from high school, and the truant officer called my house. When my dad heard the news, he told one of my friends that he was looking for me with a shotgun. I was so frightened that I did not go home for two nights.

My mother was a typical, heavy-set, Italian-American housewife who was obedient and extremely submissive to my father. She had a warm, round face, but she was not cheerful. She loved to complain. We were never close, but from the time I was a young child, she encouraged me to enter the Catholic priesthood. I believe her encouragement drew me toward the ministry, even before I heard God's call. For that I will always be grateful.

My parents never sat down and had conversations with Albert and me about school. In fact, I don't think my father or mother knew the difference between an A and a D. All my parents knew was "Were you good in school?" and "Did you pass?" Those were important questions for them, but not for me. I wanted to excel, and I was disappointed that they didn't share my interest in good grades and school activities.

When I played for our high school teams, I always used to see my friends' families there, but my family never showed up. I wanted them to be proud of me, but I never felt equal to the other kids in school because my parents didn't seem interested. They had not gone to American schools, so they couldn't understand my aspirations.

For example, I was the starting quarterback when our team played a high school in Metuchen, New Jersey. Friday night before the game, my dad and I were on the front porch. Normally I was afraid to ask him, but this time I wasn't.

"Tomorrow, I'm going to start. Would you come?"

"What time is it?"

I was surprised and pleased. *Maybe I haven't been fair to my dad,* I thought. *Maybe he really is interested.*

"Three-thirty," I said.

"OK. I'll be there."

I was really excited about the game, and throughout the pregame activities I searched the stands for my family. Several of my brothers and sisters were there, but not my dad. It was a good game, and I played well, but it didn't really mean as much because my dad wasn't there.

At home that night, I asked him why he hadn't come.

"Don't bother me with those stupid things," he growled.

Much later I would learn that he sat in a bar with his friends during the game. He felt more at ease with them than he would have at a high school game that was so foreign to him. He couldn't show enthusiasm for me because I was part of another world.

"Quit school," he would say. "You make a living with what you do with your hands, not with your brain."

Albert listened and followed his advice. He quit school, and my parents respected that decision. Because I wouldn't quit, they thought I was lazy and didn't want to work hard. It made me feel like the black sheep of the family.

Of all my brothers and sisters, I admired Joey the most. He was thirteen years older than Albert and me, and he always seemed big and strong. If I took after anybody, it was Joey. Almost everything he did backed up in his face, and he was always trying to prove himself. He quit school early and became a successful refinisher. He was the most talented of us brothers, maybe even better than Dad.

Danny liked to show off. He was a short boy and weighed only 125 pounds, but he was tough. He played all the sports and earned high school letters. He was two years younger than Joey, but he broke away from the family before anyone else when he graduated from high school and joined the Air Force. He fell in love with an English girl while in the service, and they were married. When he was discharged he started in the family business, but he pulled out after several years and became a landscaper. While in high school, I worked two summers for him and learned the landscaping business. We put in lawns, rock gardens, and so on and even designed an entire piece of property. Now Danny is in the refinishing business in Flemington, New Jersey.

Noreen was attractive. She had dark hair and a beautiful face and figure, and the boys swarmed around her. She was quiet and even-tempered, and I always felt close to her.

Michael, two years younger than Noreen and seven years older than Albert and me, was the only one who was not mechanical. He quit school at fourteen and became a greenhouse gardener. In his thirties he opened a floral arts business. He taught me how to do floral arrangements, and I often worked for him on the nights before holidays. The business did well, but Michael didn't want the burden of running a business, so he went to work for a department store. He never married, and because he lives close to my parents, he has watched after them through the years.

Cookie talked a lot and had a lot of energy. She always was in charge. Albert and I depended on her a great deal. In fact, when Cookie and her husband, Jerry, lived with the family for several years after they were married, they were our substitute parents. Their warmth and emotional support often sustained us in the squabbles and hurts of growing up. If we wanted something, Cookie would always go out of her way to convince my mother and father to do it.

Cookie kept the house and was in charge of Albert and me. She'd make us wash the dishes, dust the furniture, clean our bedrooms, and make our beds. But I could never do things well enough for her.

For example, I'd work hard to make my bed, but when she inspected it, she'd scream, ''That bed is a mess. You did a lousy job.''

I'd be looking and thinking, *Where's the lousy job?* I honestly thought it was perfect, but she'd pull the bedding up and I would have to start again.

''I'm tough on you for your own good, Tom,'' she would say.

She'd make us fold our clothes, and if they weren't just right, she'd throw the contents of the drawer on the bed. When we cleaned the dishes, if there were a spot on a dish, she'd put all the dishes back into the sink again. No matter what we did, it was never good enough, and her decision was final. We could never plead our case with Mom and Dad.

Cookie was trying to teach us to do our best no matter what the circumstances. She wanted us to do well for ourselves, not for anyone else. She thought that if we knew we did our best, no one could complain. She wanted us to establish a pattern of perfection, but that emphasis tended to intensify competition among us, and I often was depressed because of reminders that I was not good enough.

Although my parents' strict discipline may not have been the best for all of us, it did make us self-reliant. All of us learned the refinishing business at an early age.

Once when I was working in my father's refinishing shop, he told me to do a piece. When I finished he asked me, ''Is it good?''

''Yes.''

''No, it isn't,'' he said, and threw it back into the stripping vat.

I worked on the piece five times. After the fifth time I said, ''Dad, it was good. I looked at it. It was very good.''

''Was it good the first time?'' he asked.

''Yeah.''

''Did you think it was as good as it could be?''

"Yeah."

"Then why didn't you have enough confidence to stand behind it and tell me?"

"You mean you knew it was good to start with, and you threw it in the vat four times?"

"If you don't believe it's good, how can anybody else believe it's good?" he asked.

That was my father's way. He taught us discipline in ways we could never forget.

Another rule was that we couldn't sit down at the kitchen table until the elder of the house sat down first. When I was about sixteen years old, we had a big family gathering in our house. We were all standing around the table, and somehow I had the impression that my grandmother had sat down; so I sat down. Grandmother had sat down, but then she had stood up and walked into the kitchen.

When my father saw me sitting, he swung at me. "You don't have any respect for your grandmother," he shouted. "What's wrong with you?"

My father and mother insisted that we respect our elders even if they were wrong. For example, we were to be quiet and listen when an elder talked. But I never could keep quiet.

"But why?" I would ask about something.

"You're arguing, Tom," was the inevitable reply.

I went through my whole childhood saying, "I don't understand this."

"Stop arguing," my parents would say.

"I'm not trying to argue. I just want you to explain it to me."

"There you go again, you're arguing with me. Now shut up."

That's the way I grew up. They said I was always an arguer. But I was frustrated because I couldn't say anything. I couldn't even ask a question.

In other words, I just couldn't seem to fit in. I was an oddball who never could follow the rules for any length of time, and that pattern of behavior has been evident throughout my life.

Early one morning during my junior year in high school, we had finished breakfast and I was following my father up the stairs. Suddenly he seemed to waver. Then he fell. He got up and started to fall again. For a second or two I stood motionless. Then I realized he couldn't walk.

"Dad, what's wrong?" I asked.

"I'm dizzy," he mumbled. I tried to help him up the stairs and into the bedroom. He couldn't talk or move his arm. I was shaking so badly that I could hardly dial the doctor's telephone number. After getting the doctor's assurance that he would come right over, I called Mom.

The doctor arrived in a few minutes. He checked Dad out and came down to the kitchen, where we were waiting. "He's had a stroke," he said, "but I don't think it's serious. We'll take him to the hospital and place him on some medication. If he responds well, we can get him into therapy within a few weeks."

Fortunately, the prognosis was correct. Dad recovered within a few months. However, the doctor warned that the stroke, although not serious, probably was an indication of a physical weakness. He told my dad he could go back to work, but he ruled out the vigorous schedule of the prestroke years.

When my dad returned to work, he didn't pay any attention. He refused to slow down, and he had a second stroke during my senior year. I felt that I had a lot to do with it, because Dad and I had just had a shouting match moments before. Mike, Albert, Mom, Dad, and I had just finished dinner. Albert and Mike left, and Dad walked into the living room and turned on the television.

"Did you mention the prom to Dad?" I asked my mother as I carried dishes to the sink. Earlier I had asked her if I could go to the prom.

"Ask your father," she said.

Dad was laughing at an Abbott and Costello movie, obviously in a good mood. "Dad, can I go to the prom?" I asked.

"What does that have to do with me?" he said.

"I'll need some money," I explained.

"I don't have any," he said. "Ask your mother."

"But, Dad, Mom said to ask you."

"Don't argue with me," he said, and went into a tirade. I can't repeat the language he used.

"I'm sorry, Dad, I didn't know what to do," I said. "I was just doing what I thought was right."

"Stop arguing with me," he said. "I can't even watch TV in peace."

Moments later he suffered the second stroke, and this one would leave him partially disabled. It would be months before he would be able to communicate, and then only in sounds that were rough approximations of words. He never again would be able to use his marvelous skills of refinishing and upholstering. He would walk, but only with a cane.

He was fifty-four years old, and he and my mother retired to Tom's River, New Jersey, a town about eighty miles south of New York City. I stayed in Scotch Plains for several months until I graduated from high school.

I had experienced the normal amount of childhood crises during my school years, and many of them were caused by my almost intrepid sense of impulsiveness and lack of stick-to-itiveness. I always seemed to be able to wiggle free of long-term responsibilities. I knew this, and it gave me a sense of self-contempt that was expressed in the most incredible kinds of excuses. But deep down inside myself, I believed the excuses. I was convinced that my behavior was justified. However, one afternoon in September during my senior year in high school, I took the first step to face my self-centeredness.

I was walking home, down Westfield Road, with several of my friends. On one corner each day our high school history teacher would stand and tell anyone who would listen that Jesus Christ was loving and forgiving.

Most of my friends would make fun of him. They were

Roman Catholic, and they'd say, "Look at that idiot."

In Catholic catechism, we had been taught that it was wrong to talk to anyone who wasn't Catholic. In fact, we were told that the Baptist preacher was satanic. We were told we shouldn't even go into another church because we would go to hell if we did.

The lay preacher was a stocky, bald man with horn-rimmed glasses and a very meek manner. He never got upset when my friends mocked him. For some reason, I didn't react against him.

In fact, after walking past him hundreds of times during my high school days, his message finally got to me. On this day the preacher's words seemed to jump out at me.

"God loves all of us. Jesus died on the cross because He loved all men and forgave all men—even for the worst sin, even for the crime of murder."

I paid even closer attention. He seemed to be talking directly to me, and I realized for the first time that going to hell, purgatory, and mortal sin were all put aside because of Christ. I understood that Jesus really loved me enough to forgive me despite my carelessness and irresponsibility.

"Come on, Tom," one of my friends said. "If Father Nelligan catches you listening to this, he's going to be mad at you, and you may get kicked out of being an altar boy." But I just couldn't leave. I was engrossed in how loving Jesus Christ was, and I wanted to hear more.

I had been standing with a group of long-haired guys who wore black jackets and had long, slick hair like "The Fonz." They saw that I was interested in what the preacher was saying.

"Go talk with him, Scarinci," they teased.

I wouldn't, but I kept listening, and they left. After a few minutes, I walked up to the preacher and began to cry. Soon I was sobbing uncontrollably. I realized that someone really cared about me, no matter how bad I was. I didn't have to pretend to be a tough guy. I could be loved for who I was.

"He'll never forgive me," I said. "I've lied, and I've exaggerated, and I've done things wrong, and my family thinks I'm bad."

"God will forgive everything," he said. "All you have to do is ask for forgiveness and admit that you're a sinner and that you need His help. He will forgive you totally, and you will be a new creation."

The preacher put his arms around me, and we walked off the sidewalk and sat under a big elm tree that stood in front of a rambling Victorian house. As he talked, it began to rain.

He sheltered his Bible from the rain and read from John 14. Then he explained the chapter to me. "All you have to do is ask Jesus into your heart," he said.

"I believe in God," I said.

"Have you asked Him into your life?" he asked.

"No," I said.

"Do you want to?"

"Yes," I said. I wanted to accept Christ into my life, but I was scared about my church's reaction. I didn't know that the Lord was bigger than any church organization, and I wavered for several minutes. Finally I put aside my fears, and we knelt in the rain on that corner in Scotch Plains while I prayed.

It took me years to understand what had happened. I didn't grow spiritually for a long time, but it was a beginning. I had made a decision to receive Jesus, and over time, God was going to deal with me until I submitted totally to His power and love.

Nevertheless, I was scared to death to tell anyone, much less my parents. I knew my family believed Protestants would go to hell, and I lived in fear that they would find out. If they had known it, my parents would have been totally humiliated, even though they were not regular churchgoers.

I lived with the dread that they would find out, until Noreen married Neil McCallum, a big, handsome Scotsman who was Presbyterian. They had a Presbyterian wedding, and Neil and his mother talked with me about the Lord.

Later, I asked Noreen if Protestants would go to heaven. "If we believe in Jesus Christ is what counts," she said, "not whether we are Protestant or Catholic."

Then I felt free to tell Noreen of that decision for Christ during my senior year.

Soon after graduation, I would establish a pattern of moving from one job to another and one crisis to another. I would be driven to become somebody. I would all but forget my commitment to the Lord in my frantic search for my family's approval and success and happiness, yet my activities were merely a symptom of my restlessness.

I moved to Tom's River after graduation to help take care of my parents, but I felt somewhat ambivalent. I now had a lot more freedom to come and go, but I no longer could lose myself in the world of extracurricular activities. I had a responsibility to earn a living because of my dad's disability, and I would not be able to go to college full-time. I took night courses in psychology and physical education at Rutgers University, and I signed up for correspondence work at LaSalle Extension School.

Something was missing from my life. Fortunately, I learned that church officials were starting a new high school in the Tom's River area, and in conversations with Father Herbert Stopp, I explored possibilities that would enable me to go to school part-time and work.

"As long as you continue in school with us and you want to go into the ministry, you can teach here," Father Stopp said.

I thought this was a great opportunity because I had been encouraged to work for the church, and I considered the ministry seriously. Now I could prepare for the ministry with Father Stopp and Father Callihan, vicar of the church, learning the liturgical aspect of the priesthood and studying orders.

It may be difficult for Protestants to understand how someone who had given his life to Jesus could continue in the Roman Catholic Church, with all its ecclesiastical trappings and questionable doctrines, and even study for its priesthood.

It wasn't difficult for me. I was raised in a strong Italian family whose very life was so intertwined with Catholicism that our family history could not be told without including a lot about the church. Most of the people I knew were Catholics. To leave those friendships would be to deny who I was, an impressionable teenager who had always felt pressure to conform to family wishes.

But I did not conform readily. That was one of my problems. I always seemed to be questioning family mores. Also, I did feel a great deal of conflict between my faith and the ritual of the Catholic Church and the fear it induced in its followers.

Father Callihan told me that the Lord is forgiving, but that unless we live with the fear of God in us, we will sin terribly. That was a religion without freedom, and eventually I would break away from it. But that would not happen until my life became so desperate that I would have to move to the other side of the country and begin again.

After several months the mother superior approached me. "Tom, we've got a problem," she said. "We've got a lot of students failing algebra. What we'd like to do is form a general science class for them. How would you like to teach it?"

"Sure," I said. I was eager for new challenges. I also was handling the Catholic Youth Organization (CYO) basketball program for our district in the state of New Jersey. These supervisory activities were increased when an additional building was made available for us. I started an exercise program, a dance program, and a club for Friday and Saturday nights. We were serving the youth in the area, whether they were Catholic or not.

3

The New Life

I was at the center of a whirlwind of activity, and I was happy because my mother was in total support of my teaching at St. Joseph's and preparing for the ministry. Both my parents wanted me to make something of myself, and they thought being on the faculty of St. Joseph's was prestigious. However, during the year they realized that there was little money in church work. Their enthusiasm seemed to wane, and I grew restless.

I wanted to go to school full-time and work part-time to pay my bills, so I forgot about the ministry. The lure of money and a good time was too strong. I applied for a part-time job in the men's clothing department at Britt's Department Store in Britt's Township and was hired. I learned my responsibilities quickly and enjoyed the work immensely—so much, in fact, that I decided not to go to school full-time when my boss offered me the job full-time. Obviously, I had no clear goals. I was merely responding to the opportunity of the moment and the path of least resistance. The irresponsible self-centeredness that dominated my life was encouraged by my successes. I was named manager of the clothing department. Then my brother helped me get an interview at Klein's Department Store in Edison, New Jersey, where he was the assistant manager of the florist department.

On the day I was interviewed for the job, I joked with a young lady named Eileen who was working in the business office. She was a slim, talkative blonde with blue eyes, and I could tell she liked me. Every place I went in the store during that day, I'd see her. I couldn't seem to avoid meeting her. I walked down the stairs, and she said hello. Then, as I was leaving, she was going out the door, too. I turned around and asked her, "Are you following me or something?"

"No, I thought you were following me," she said coyly.

"Well, since we're both going the same way, why don't we have lunch together?"

A few days later, I was hired to work in the housewares department at Klein's. Within three or four months, I was made assistant manager and then manager. Meanwhile, Eileen and I began dating.

As the relationship between us grew, I began to realize that Eileen loved me, and I knew she would marry me. We talked about marriage, and soon we announced our engagement. But our plans were interrupted late in the fall of 1963 when I received a draft notice. The United States was already involved in Vietnam in an advisory capacity, and I didn't think I would get much training in the Army. So I went to the Air Force recruiting office and enlisted.

Six months later, I received an honorable discharge from active duty so that I could help support my disabled parents. I had not enjoyed the military; I was disappointed by the lack of discipline.

But returning to civilian life did not give me a sense of direction, either. I was lonely. I was the only one in the family who was single. Even my brother Albert was married. In fact, he and his wife were expecting a child. I wanted someone to love and talk to. I wanted to have a relationship that would keep me from ever feeling lonely again, so Eileen and I made final our marriage plans. Cookie realized why I was marrying and that I didn't love Eileen, and she tried to tell me it wouldn't work. But I wouldn't listen, and Eileen and I were married on October 4, 1964.

I can't say that we ever were happy in our marriage. From the day of our wedding there was no joy in our relationship. She could feel that I didn't love her. As a result, our relationship moved from neutral to bad. There was no peace. It was another example of my acting selfishly and impetuously, without consulting God.

Eileen and I had two sons within two years, and I loved them both deeply. In spite of that, our relationship never grew, and gradually she seemed to lose interest in me and the boys. I eventually discovered that she was being unfaithful to me, and although I wanted to patch up our marriage, she refused. Finally, she left with the boys, and I was never able to find her. My marriage, a mistake from the beginning, ended in divorce.

My failure in marriage led me to severe depression many times, and more than once I attempted suicide. I was the only one in my family whose marriage didn't work out, and I felt totally worthless. In one suicide attempt, I repeatedly smashed my face against a bathroom mirror, cutting myself badly, because I hated the image of the loser I considered myself to be.

By the time I was released from the hospital following my last attempt, I realized I had to get away from everything that reminded me of my past. I knew my life was a mess, but I couldn't understand that a major source of my problem was spiritual. I had not made Jesus Lord of my life.

Sometimes my sense of failure was so great that I felt I couldn't breathe, and I was so ashamed of myself. I pleaded with God to bring Eileen back so that I could make up with her. In my grief, I met a young woman in our neighborhood who was a waitress in a coffee shop where I stopped every morning on the way to work at my brother's shop. I learned that she was going to visit her mother in California, and I asked if I could drive to

California with her. With only a few belongings, I set off in mid-1970 on the cross-country drive.

When we got there, we went our separate ways. I began to live in Carmichael, but it was a miserable existence. I dreaded facing each day, and I no longer wanted to overcome my problems. I tried everything I could to escape from myself. I even tried to read the Bible, but I never got anything out of it. During those months I met Joy, a beautiful woman from Louisiana. She had long, black hair and dark brown eyes, and when she looked at me I was almost hypnotized. Her deep southern accent and her soft manners helped me forget my failures, and we started dating. It became apparent that we needed each other. She told me her husband had walked out on her, but she wasn't serious about a long-term relationship. She merely wanted to live with me.

"I can't live that way," I said. "I wasn't brought up that way." I had also already experienced too much hurt. I didn't want any more.

She'd tell me how much she loved me, and that she never knew anyone like me. However, I didn't love her and was afraid I might not be able to get out of the relationship if I let it continue much longer. My solution was to move to San Jose, where I started taking courses at San Jose State University. I found a job as the chief consultant with the Beltone Hearing Center in San Jose. Patients were referred to me for therapy by doctors in the area, and gradually my practice built up until I was doing extremely well.

Meanwhile, Joy learned that I had moved to the San Jose area and came to see me during the summer of 1971. Because I was lonely and she had made such an effort to see me, I began to go out with her again, and she moved to San Jose. We were having a great time, and I began to think about marriage. I was making another mistake, namely, thinking about marrying someone just because I was lonely and wanted someone to talk to.

Clearly, I had not learned my lessons. I still thought only in terms of immediate gratification.

Nevertheless, my naive plans were shattered when I was hospitalized with an apparent heart attack. Fortunately, I had not had a heart attack; I was merely exhausted.

When the doctor came in the morning after the attack, he told me he was going to move me to another hospital.

"But I don't have any money," I said.

"Use this," he said, and handed me a twenty-dollar bill. "Then we'll see what we can do to help you out."

I took a cab and stayed at the new hospital a couple of days, until the administrator learned they couldn't get any medical aid for me. Then I was released from the hospital.

When the doctor learned that I had no place to stay, he suggested the crisis prevention center in San Jose. It was a county center set up like a halfway house for ex-addicts and people who were suicidal. He didn't think I would like to stay there too long, but it would be a good place for me between the time I got out of the hospital and the time I located a place to live. When I arrived at the crisis center, I explained my situation to one of the head supervisors. She said she would take care of me when she finished eating, and she asked me to join the staff and patients for dinner.

I walked into the dining room, where twenty to twenty-five people were sitting at a long table. The supervisor asked me to sit at the end of one side of the table. As I began to help myself to the food, I noticed a beautiful, blue-eyed blonde across the table at the other end. The expression on her face seemed to say, "I wonder what's wrong with him," as she occasionally glanced my way with a smile on her face. It seemed she could tell I was depressed, and apparently she wanted to encourage me; so she walked up to me after the meal. She was wearing hunter green trousers, a white blouse, and a green vest. She looked gorgeous, and her blonde hair accented her warm smile.

The supervisor introduced her as Cheryl Friesen. We talked

for several minutes, and I asked her if she would take a walk with me. As we walked, I told her what had happened to me, and we discussed counseling. She told me about the problems at the crisis center. She said I didn't have the kinds of problems common to the patients there, and that I shouldn't stay.

Then Cheryl went back to her room while I leaned on the railing of the brick front steps. She brought back her guitar and sat down in the middle of the steps. As she strummed and looked at me, she communicated a depth and vitality I had never known. Although we had known each other only an hour or two, I felt very close to Cheryl, and I made a major decision. When she stopped playing, I looked at her and said:

> You are a perfect woman,
> A dream that is everlasting.
> By day my life begins with you,
> By night you are part of me;
> For you are the beauty of today
> And the joys of tomorrow.

I leaned over and kissed her on the forehead. "If I see you again, young lady," I said, "I'm going to marry you." She burst out laughing. Here was some guy she had known for only a few hours, showing off by spouting poetry and talking about marrying her. It was ridiculous. *Nobody spontaneously makes up poetry like that,* she thought. *Who's he trying to impress?* But when she stopped laughing, I knew she was beginning to understand me. She kept looking at me as if she were asking herself whether it really could happen.

I stayed at the center that night, and the next morning Cheryl wanted to help me find a place to stay. I found an apartment complex in San Jose that was owned and managed by Jim Cojanis, a short, wiry-looking fellow with black hair who was very set in his ways. We talked for several minutes, and I learned that Jim had grown up in Westville, New Jersey. In fact, I used to eat in his father's restaurant in Plainfield, and my father built the bar counter for that restaurant. I later learned that

Jim was a traditional Catholic until he became a Pentecostal Catholic. This development in his faith would one day have a great impact on me and Cheryl.

Cheryl was an extremely talented person. Her father had directed various construction projects throughout the world. He was an instrumentation engineer with a big corporation and he had provided her with an excellent education. She had studied medicine and psychology at the University of Vienna, where Sigmund Freud once taught. Her specialty was going to be psychosomatic medicine.

I liked Cheryl, and I knew she liked me. On the very first day she let me drive her canary yellow Volkswagen, something she didn't let anyone else do. She was very particular about letting anyone have anything of hers. Although I knew she liked me, however, she had told me that her only interest was a professional career, and that she had no intentions of getting married.

The next morning we tried to get my apartment set up, and we stopped for lunch at a place in Los Gatos.

"What's happening may be a dream," I told her, "but we may never see each other again." I wanted her to understand how real my feelings were, but also how the attraction may be just a passing thing. She started crying, and I did, too. At that point my life was so confused, and I didn't want to misrepresent myself to her.

After lunch we drove to Vasona Park and walked hand in hand in the shade of the giant trees along a gentle river. We had been there a while when I realized I did not have my glasses, and I got up to look for them. I looked for a long time before I gave up and leaned against a tree. Cheryl looked at me, and then slowly she leaned toward me and kissed me. "You know, I love you," she said softly.

"Cheryl—" I was having trouble saying what I wanted to say.

"Say it, Tom," Cheryl said.

"I love you, too."

I wasn't sure of myself at that time, but something made me say that.

There was a magic about what happened. It didn't just happen. Here I had worked so hard at making relationships, and then, without any effort, I had felt love. Repeatedly I was seeing God's action in my life, and slowly it was dawning on me that no matter how much I wanted to control my own life, the Lord gradually was taking over.

A short time later I became very sick, so I stayed with Cheryl and her girlfriend in Santa Clara. Cheryl's love and care drew us close, and I proposed. Almost immediately she called her mom and dad and told them about me. They were shocked. They never expected her to get married, especially after all the education she had gone through to be a professional person. But Cheryl had made her plans.

"Mom, we're going to have a new wedding," she said.

I listened as they talked, and a few minutes later they ended the conversation.

"My mom sure seemed upset," she said as the phone rang again almost immediately.

It was Cheryl's father. "What are you talking about, having a nude wedding?" he asked. "What kind of guy is this?"

Cheryl's mother thought Cheryl had said "nude" wedding instead of "new." I had to get on the phone and explain what we were going to do, but it took five or ten minutes for me to calm them down.

Shortly after that, Cheryl decided it was time to introduce me to her parents. Her dad was working on construction of a refinery in Bellingham, Washington. We planned to be with them during Thanksgiving, and in late November 1971 we drove through northern California, Oregon, and Washington on snowy highways to Bellingham, which is almost on the Canadian border. When we arrived at her parents' apartment, Cheryl introduced me. We had been there only a few moments when Mr. Friesen said, "Tom, I'd like to take a ride with you."

It was an abrupt way to be greeted, but there was nothing I could do but take the drive. When we got in the car, he started interrogating me. I felt I was on trial, and it made me nervous. However, I became really angry when he wanted to know how much money I had in the bank.

"With all due respect to you, Mr. Friesen," I said, "it's none of your business what I've got in my bank account. But if you want to know if I can support your daughter, yes, I'll do everything I can to give her everything she desires. I love your daughter, and I guarantee I'll take care of her." He respected my answer, and I began to feel more relaxed as we drove back to the apartment.

Approximately two months after I moved into one of Jim's rental units, he took a Christmas vacation, visiting his brother in Tucson, Arizona. He asked me to watch his eight apartment units because he didn't have a manager, and he left a phone number for me to call in case of an emergency. Little did I realize what problems I would have. On Christmas Eve there was a tremendous rainstorm, and, because one of Jim's tenants left big holes in the roof when he had taken down his television antenna, three apartments were flooded. Somehow I got a roofer to repair the roof the next day, and I was able to calm the tenants.

When Jim returned, he was grateful for my efforts to protect his property, and we became very good friends. His brother, John, had been involved in the Catholic charismatic movement and often prayed for people to be healed. John and Jim regularly talked on the phone about these things. Jim described those conversations to Cheryl and me, but he seemed a little overbearing, and I thought he was too zealous about reading the Bible, going to hear different evangelists, and listening to tape cassettes.

Despite how well things were going with Cheryl and me, I was worried. I was so insecure because I had had so many bad experiences with women that I didn't want anything to happen that would hurt me again. I didn't want to be misled, and I was afraid to make a commitment because I was afraid Cheryl would back out and not love me. I was remembering my first marriage. I was afraid to love unconditionally. I didn't want to be hurt, but at the same time, I had nowhere to go. I needed that love from somebody.

Nonetheless, in spite of all my fears, all my hatred, and all my hurt, I believed that God created Cheryl for me. I wanted her to love me the same way I loved her—in spite of my mistakes. I had a fear at that time that she'd find out some of the dumb things I had done and might not love me any more.

I wanted Cheryl to know that no matter how much we loved each other, we might go through sorrows, and the only way we could make it through those times was for her to think of me first, just as I would always think of her before myself. That way, nothing could ever separate us, because we would always be thinking of the other one first.

Cheryl had picked out her wedding dress in Bellingham before we returned to California, and we were constantly discussing the wedding and where we were going to live.

The days seemed to fly by, and as I realized more and more the importance of this decision, I started to become tense. I believed I was a failure, and I couldn't believe something so good was happening to me. I was afraid she was going to wake up that morning and believe somebody's story about me, and that would be the end of it all.

4

Drawn toward Home

For decades, Highway 9 was the only road over the Santa Cruz Mountains from the city of San Jose west to the oceanside resort of Santa Cruz. Cheryl and I often drove along that road as we explored the beauty of the historic area around Mount Hermon, the internationally known Bible conference center in the big redwood forest near Henry Coswell State Park. During one such excursion two months or so before we were married, we drove through the little town of Felton, where we saw a small aluminum structure built into the front of a quaint, reddish barn edged with white colonial trim. The sign said "Bertacelli's Upholstery."

The name and the business intrigued me, and I eased the car off the pavement onto the gravel parking area and stopped.

"Cheryl, wouldn't it be nice if we could have a little place like that?" I asked.

"Are you crazy?" she said. "We don't have any money. How can we buy anything?"

I was doing well in counseling and in audiology, but I had long felt that my father was disappointed because I had not entered the family decorating and furniture refinishing business that had existed for generations. The thought of my own business really intrigued me.

I turned the engine off and opened the door. "Come on. Let's go in and talk to Mr. Bertacelli," I said.

"About what?" Cheryl asked.

"Going back to my grandfather," I said with a smile.

Cheryl was surprised because we had never talked about my interest in a family decorating business. I had told her that my family is known for upholstery work, handcrafting of furniture, marble cutting, and diamond cutting. My ancestors made wine bottles for the Vatican and did many other forms of craft work. In fact, a town in the province of Ciatta, Italy, was named after my family. But I had only mentioned this in passing, and Cheryl had no way of knowing how deep my interests were. Moreover, I never considered the possibility of entering the business until I saw Bertacelli's sign.

I walked over to the side of the store, and Cheryl followed me. The barn and store stood about twenty feet off the highway on the side of a hill that slowly eased down to the San Lorenzo River. Our eyes took in a rustic, wooden fence that surrounded the lot and plum trees that clustered in a small orchard near the back. There wasn't much traffic on Highway 9, and we could hear the bubbling sounds of the river. Its slow, sparkling stream happily accented this peaceful plot of ground on the edge of the jungle of highways, shopping malls, neon signs, and pleasure-seeking activity that is the resort area of Santa Cruz County. The property reminded me of the small farmhouse and lot on which I had grown up in New Jersey, and I felt drawn to it as if it were meant for me.

We turned, walked slowly to the front door, and entered a surprisingly large display area filled with upholstery material and old furniture, some needing to be reupholstered and some already repaired. Through an open door to the left, I could see what looked like a small apartment.

"Can I help you?" a tall, balding man in a green plaid sportshirt asked.

"We're looking for Mr. Bertacelli," I said.

"That's me," he announced in a voice richly flavored by years of Mediterranean culture.

"I saw your sign, and it reminded me of my family," I said. "I'm Tom Scarinci. Back in Italy they pronounce it 'Skarinji.' This is my fiancée, Cheryl."

His eyes sparkled, and I knew he liked me. We were fellow Italians.

"My father and his brothers came from the old country with the family business," I said. "My grandfather and great-grandfather and great-great-grandfather ran the business for generations. So my father and my uncles continued the tradition in New Jersey. They introduced my brothers and cousins and myself to the business as soon as we started school. We'd come home and spend a couple of hours in the shop each afternoon."

Mr. Bertacelli beamed. Not only was I Italian, but I came from the same guild, or craft, as he did. We were like family, and he showed me around his shop.

He was retired, but he kept the business open on a part-time basis, doing only upholstery work. After going through the display area and the work area, we walked into the barn. It was huge, and he used only part of it for storing furniture that needed repair. In my mind I envisioned a well-equipped refinishing shop while Mr. Bertacelli described his years in the business. It could be used for woodworking, I thought, and there was an area that could easily be converted into a refinishing room for spraying varnish and paint. The place had almost limitless potential.

Mr. Bertacelli led the way as we walked back into the display area, and there was a lull in the conversation as he reflected on our discussion. He had shown me around, and he had learned that my family had taught me the business inside and out. Now he seemed to be thinking, hoping I would want to be part of the business and almost feeling I would ask.

"Mr. Bertacelli," I said. He stopped and turned toward me. "You're going to think I'm crazy, but we're going to move into the area, and I'd like to buy your business. You could keep on working part-time with me, and I could take some of the responsibilities off you. And we could both continue our families' traditions.''

He liked the idea. We talked for several minutes and settled on a price, $2,500. I would put down $500, all my savings in the bank, and pay him the remaining $2,000 within thirty days. During that time, he would let me work out of the shop.

Mr. Bertacelli seemed exuberant. His eyes almost wrinkled shut as he beamed a broad smile, and we shook hands. We were Italians. We were brothers. We understood. The handshake was more binding than any signed contract. It represented honor and tradition, generations of craftsmen whose handshakes had been a guarantee that they would live up to their promises. Now we would be working together.

Cheryl had been silent throughout. She is somewhat shy until she gets to know a person, and when she's bothered by something, she just keeps quiet. That's the way she was as Bertacelli and I talked.

I could feel her uncertainty. She had thought I liked counseling and audiology. She knew very little about my past interests in upholstery, and I had shown little interest in it during our courtship. Now I had seen a sign beside a highway, and suddenly I couldn't think of anything else. All I wanted to do was upholstery work, and I was willing to risk everything I owned to buy an upholstery business.

I knew she couldn't understand my enthusiasm, but I moved ahead with the negotiations anyway. I knew the business was just what we both wanted. I was convinced that Cheryl would look back on this decision as a stroke of genius. She just didn't know how much I knew about that kind of work.

We said good-bye to Mr. Bertacelli and got back in the car, and Cheryl was still quiet. I had started the engine and eased back onto the highway before she spoke. ''Is that what you really want, Tom?'' she asked.

''Yeah. It'll make my father proud of me. And I'd enjoy getting into it for a while. There's good money in it.''

"But you heard Mr. Bertacelli," she said anxiously. "He's not really making that kind of money in this area."

"There's no one in this area who knows what I know about this kind of business," I replied. "I can do many things. I'm also an appraiser. And it'll be a good start for us. We'll be in the mountains, in a small town, away from everybody."

That purchase was a good example of my impulsiveness. I just didn't take all the details and ramifications of such a transaction into account. I merely jumped into action without thinking. In fact, when I look back on it, I often wonder how I could have seriously considered such a purchase. Within an hour after seeing a store sign, I had made an agreement to put all my savings into a business and throw my time and energy into the effort to pay $2,000 within thirty days while holding another job.

I didn't consult my bride-to-be. I didn't talk to my current employer. I didn't pray about it. I just did it. I thought it would prove to everybody, particularly my family, that I could make it without anybody's help—that I was somebody.

"You're crazy," Cheryl said as we drove down the highway. "Only you could walk in off the street with no money in your pocket and walk out owning a business."

I took her words as a compliment because she was so accepting of me, but I shouldn't have. She was describing a serious flaw in my personality.

At the time, I wasn't a part of any church. Similarly, Cheryl was not close to any church fellowship. Although she had grown up in a Christian home, she was leery of church people and did not worship regularly.

In our transaction, Mr. Bertacelli had provided a place for me to do woodworking and furniture refinishing in the barn. I quit my other job and went out with him on some of his calls for upholstery work. Usually I would talk a customer into letting me refinish the furniture also, so payment for that part of the work was subtracted from my $2,000 debt.

After I had several jobs lined up, I bought compressors and spray guns and set up a total refinishing business. I worked long hours, but I made good money and had paid my debt to Mr. Bertacelli within the thirty days. He would work for several months and then retire.

There is good profit in the refinishing business because the customer pays for craftsmanship. If I did $2,000 worth of work on a table, the materials might cost as much as $500, but no more than that. All the rest was labor. It may sound as though I was taking advantage of customers, but I did good work, and a $2,000 refinishing job might make the table worth $5,000.

Cheryl and I were deeply in love. We spent hours talking about our lives together, discussing our dreams and hopes. During those times, we made plans for the wedding and wrote our own ceremony.

We wanted something unique. We reserved a beautiful villa for March 4, 1972, at the Villa Montalvo Center of the Arts, a large estate where concerts and art shows are held. It's in Saratoga, on a hilltop overlooking the entire Santa Clara Valley.

Cheryl kept reminding me to memorize my vows. "Memorize your vows," she repeatedly urged, "and don't forget what you're supposed to say." Ironically, after all those reminders, Cheryl was the one who forgot her vows. She failed to say "for better or for worse." So, when we have some crisis today, she teases me, "I never promised in my wedding vows that I'd go through worse with you."

After the vows, Cheryl played her guitar and sang "Suzanne," a song about a lonely person who's "down by the river" and who depends on God. At the end of the ceremony she played "Let It Be." That song declared that no one could interfere with our love, no matter what happened. That night I gave her a gold charm. I wanted her to remember that whatever our life together would bring, she was one person I was never going to desert. My love would be permanent.

Our difficulties began almost immediately, within twenty-four hours, on our honeymoon in Monterey, California. We had just checked in at an exclusive, rustic resort on the ocean, and we returned to the desk in the lobby to have the innkeeper cash a check for us.

Cheryl signed the check, and the woman routinely put it through Tellcheck, a national system for determining whether checks are valid.

The woman returned to the counter, holding the check out to Cheryl. "I'm sorry," she told Cheryl, "but there are several unpaid checks under your name."

Cheryl's face was unchanged. She looked at the innkeeper as if she hadn't heard her words. Actually, she didn't understand what the woman was telling us.

"What do you mean?" she asked.

"Mrs. Scarinci, you cashed some checks with insufficient funds."

Cheryl's eyes showed uncertainty, then hurt and a tinge of fear. She turned to me. "What does she mean?"

"I don't know," I answered. I was confused, too.

The assistant innkeeper explained the situation to us again.

Gradually it occurred to me that Joy must have stolen and cashed some of my checks. "Cheryl, this must have to do with Joy," I said. "She must have used my name and cashed some stolen checks."

"But she said your 'wife,' " Cheryl persisted. "We've only been married a few hours."

"Joy must have signed the checks as Mrs. Tom Scarinci," I said.

Cheryl was bewildered and somewhat angry, but we agreed that the lobby was no place to discuss an important family problem, and we went back to our room. We had reserved a large room overlooking the ocean. It was furnished with antiques and deep burgundy carpets and draperies, and there was a big fireplace.

"Don't be angry, Cheryl," I said. "I didn't know anything about this, and I'm as hurt as you are."

"How can you expect me not to be angry when some woman ruins our honeymoon by signing checks as Mrs. Tom Scarinci? I wonder how many more are out there."

It really was unfair to Cheryl. I hadn't told her much about Joy, so as far as Cheryl was concerned, an unknown person was keeping us from enjoying our honeymoon.

We had planned to stay at the resort for several days, but I called the credit bureau and learned there were $450 in checks written against my former bank account in Santa Clara. I told Cheryl, and after a long talk in which she expressed her deep hurt, we concluded that our honeymoon would have to be shortened. We didn't have much cash, and we couldn't sign any checks. We had to return home after two days.

What a way to start a honeymoon! What a way to start a marriage! Not only did we have to come back early, but I also had bills to pay on bad checks. In fact, we used our wedding money to pay the checks. I felt so badly for Cheryl, who had to be shortchanged because of my errors before she met me.

When we returned to Felton, we rented a little place in the mountains on Lakeside Drive, and the refinishing business began to boom. I changed the name of the shop to Scarinci Brothers so that customers would know the business was under new management. I had been motivated to buy the business because of the Scarinci Brothers Shop in New Jersey. I was proud of my family's accomplishments and knew they would be proud of me for getting into the business and naming it after the original business. I asked them for authorization to use the name "Scarinci Brothers," and it was granted.

About this time, the husband of one of Cheryl's girlfriends asked Cheryl if I would consider taking him into the business with me. Cheryl had worked with his wife, and Cheryl and she thought it would help him "find" himself if he became part of our business. He was unhappy in his work and had been looking for another position for some time.

It sounded like a good idea to me. I wanted the business to grow, and an additional person could help it do just that. I knew he didn't have any background in the business, but he said he wanted to learn.

"I'll put $2,000 into the business and a truck," he offered.

How could I lose, I thought, and gave an affirmative answer. "The business will make money," I told him. "We can net twenty-five or thirty dollars an hour."

"OK," he said.

"Fine. We'll go fifty-fifty," I said.

He left his job and came to work with me. For three months business expanded slowly, and I put all my energies into it. We got into selling drapery and carpeting in addition to doing reupholstery and refinishing. We were a complete decorating service for the Santa Cruz area.

Yet my new partner and I did not seem to be compatible. Almost from the first week, I realized he would have difficulty. For example, I'd give him a job that should have taken only six hours, but it would take him three days. He was a good, slow worker, and his slowness was even more evident when he started having marital problems and talking about them at the shop. Soon he realized the partnership was not working out.

He was very unhappy, and one evening after Mr. Bertacelli had left the shop, he walked into the little back room where I was writing up a job estimate. He didn't spend much time on chit-chat but came right to the point. He wanted to do appraising work and make estimates as I did. He thought he was doing dirty work, and I was taking it easy. I tried to explain to him that it took years to develop a skill at appraisal work, and I reminded him that I usually spent three or four hours working in the shop during the evening.

But I wasn't persuasive. He thought that he should be selling and we should hire someone else to do the labor. I knew then that our problems were insurmountable, but I still hoped he would eventually be happy; and quite honestly, I just didn't want to think that things would not work out. I was determined to make the partnership a success.

On the surface the situation remained about the same, but within two weeks he told me he wanted to leave the partnership. His statement really surprised me, although it shouldn't have. We had talked many times, but I just had not taken him seriously enough. I was not prepared to end the partnership. I had counted on the continued expansion of the business and had borrowed to build an inventory of drapery and carpeting.

"How much would you like to buy me out for?" he asked.

"I'll give you back what you gave me, about four thousand dollars," I said.

"No, I can't do that," he said.

"All right, what do you want?" I asked.

"Look, we're friends. Why don't I just go to an attorney and let our attorneys handle it."

That last statement really upset Cheryl when I told her about it. After my partner first showed signs of unhappiness with the partnership, Cheryl had talked to our attorney and learned what the impact would be. "He's going to go to an attorney and he's going to find out that as a partner, if you're making money you get half of it, but if you're in debt $20,000, then you have to pay half of it," Cheryl said.

That's exactly what happened. He left work a little early one afternoon and went to his attorney, who told him he would have to pay $10,000 to get out. That news stunned him, and he seemed deep in thought as he left the shop after work.

About four o'clock the next morning, I was awakened by the phone. A man who was renting an apartment near the store told me my shop had been broken into.

I thanked him, hung up, and called the Santa Clara County

Sheriff's Department. Cheryl and I scrambled into our clothes and drove as fast as we could to the shop.

We arrived just before the sheriff. Someone had broken into the store and stolen all our equipment, some of our upholstery materials, and several antiques. The electric wires had been cut, and kerosene had been poured over everything. The deputy sheriff took a quick look and talked with the person who had called me. Then the deputy went to his squad car and used his radio to issue an all-points bulletin for two pickup trucks carrying equipment and antique furniture. Then he asked the dispatcher to call the forestry department.

Three men arrived within ten minutes and began an inspection. They determined that someone had intended to burn the shop, but a neighbor had heard the commotion and had tried to investigate. In the process, he stumbled and made some noise that frightened the intruders, and they fled before lighting the kerosene.

By the time we heard the foresters' report, several men had been apprehended driving a couple of trucks over the mountains toward San Jose. One of them was my partner. Charges were made, and my partner and his friends were arrested for burglary and attempted arson.

That whole incident was really discouraging. I had begun to build up a lot of work, and now all my compressors, my generator, and all the spray guns and sanders had been stolen, and the sheriff's office was holding everything as evidence. I called my attorney every day, asking him about the equipment, and through his efforts the equipment was returned after a month.

Meanwhile, the robbery was reported in the local newspaper, and customers were afraid their antiques had been damaged. Our phone rang off the hook. Customers wanted to forget about the job. Others wanted to know when they could have their jobs finished. Some wanted to know whether we had insurance.

We didn't, but fortunately, not much of the furniture was

damaged. Nevertheless, I purchased insurance almost immediately. We couldn't be sure we would be as fortunate some other time.

I took losses on many jobs, handing them out to other refinishers and upholsterers. It also was a risk because some of the refinishers did not do a good job. One job had to be redone three times before I was satisfied with it.

By this time my partner was going to trial. I tried to look at his situation realistically. He was getting involved extramaritally, and he had one child in his care. Obviously, it would not help his situation for him to go to jail. He needed help, and if he went to jail, he would lose everything.

"Tom, how long are you going to go on being a nice guy?" Gary Britton, my attorney, asked when I discussed the subject with him. "Good guys don't last long. You've got to stop letting people take advantage of you."

I didn't think I was being soft. I knew my partner. When the trial date came, I stood up as a character witness for him, and he didn't go to jail. Later, I heard he had become a Christian. I don't know if my action played a part in his decision, but I know his conversion was a confirmation to me that I had done the right thing by defending him.

Nevertheless, Cheryl and I were facing a major crisis. The business was on the verge of collapse. I did the only thing I could do. I started working twice as hard, day and night, trying to build things back up. Within two months after the burglary, the business had made up for the losses. It was July 1972, and I was beginning to feel I was somebody. Within six months I had started a new life. I had married a beautiful, young, sophisticated woman, and now, despite a robbery and the departure of a disgruntled partner, our new business was booming. Foolishly I began to act as though I could do anything, not realizing my survival had not been based on anything I had done. That's when I had a serious accident.

My assistant and I were delivering a sofa to an old house in a country setting. We carried it up the stairs, lifting it over a railing, and propped one end on the railing. I held the other end while my assistant went back to the truck for a screwdriver and hammer so that we could take a door off the hinges to get the sofa through. It seemed he was taking forever. I shifted the weight of the sofa and waited. But still he didn't return, and I was growing tired and impatient. Impulsively, I tried to lift the sofa myself. As I did, I leaned against the railing. I felt it give and tried to pull back, but the force of my weight and that of the sofa broke the railing, and I fell to the landing as the sofa tumbled down the stairs.

I jarred my head and neck, but it didn't hurt too much at first. However, when I tried to get out of the pickup when we arrived back at the shop, I could only turn my head slowly, and I was so stiff I could hardly straighten my legs. After a couple of days it got worse, and I went to the hospital under the care of Dr. Gail Magid.

To try to find where the damage was, Dr. Magid ordered a myelogram test. That frightened me, because I had undergone a myelogram years before when I was in a car accident as a teenager. I knew what I was going to go through. A doctor would insert a big hypodermic needle into my spinal cord to drain my spinal fluid, and at the same time he would replace the fluid with dye using another hypodermic needle that also was inserted in my spinal cord. I would be strapped on a table that enabled the doctors to turn me upside down and then all the way back the other way to distribute the dye throughout the spinal area. Then I would be turned and tipped into various positions on a table under a fluoroscope. Pictures would be taken of my back, and the doctors would be able to see the extent of damage to my spinal cord.

When the time came for the test, I was placed on my side, and a nurse inserted something in my mouth. "Bite," she said while she held my head. Another nurse held my legs, and the doctor carefully inserted the needle. Calcium buildup around my spine was so thick, however, that he had to apply pressure to force it, and I screamed. But still he failed to penetrate the spinal cord, and I jerked in reaction to the pain.

Again Dr. Magid inserted the needle, and again he was not successful.

I don't know how many times he tried, but every time he shoved, I could feel the pressure even though I had been given a local anesthetic. The needle would slip into a nerve, and pain would shoot down my leg. He'd shove again, and I'd scream out and cry like a baby.

"When's it going to be over?" I pleaded. "Please stop."

Somehow, Dr. Magid was finally successful. The needles were in place. I can't tell you how relieved I felt. But it seemed to take forever to get the X rays taken. Then the doctors began to remove the dye. They tilted me every conceivable way to get it all out. I felt like a seasick sailor on a slow-motion ship, but if dye is left in the spinal cord, more damage can be done. So, despite my discomfort, I wanted the doctors to be sure to get it all out.

Then the ordeal was completed, and I was wheeled back to my room. Usually patients have unpleasant aftereffects from a myelogram, but the only thing I felt was the continuing throb from my back injury.

The next morning, Dr. Magid walked briskly into my room. "How are you feeling?" he asked.

I mumbled something, and he said, "We found the problem, and we're going to operate on it."

He didn't ask me if I wanted the operation. He merely said he was going to do it. He even told me the day and time.

It was a rather simple procedure, he said. He would take a bone from my hip and place it in my neck. "Ninety percent of these operations are successful," he said. "Seven percent of them sometimes have a problem later, and there's a three or four percent chance that you will go out the way you came in."

I don't remember my response, but when he apparently saw

no adverse reaction from me, he continued, ''I also have to talk about death. It can happen. I don't know how many cases like yours I've done, but I haven't lost one of them. So don't worry about death.''

I didn't. I was sure I'd come through, but I was worried that I could come out of the surgery and still have the pain. I thought the pain was psychosomatic, and that I really didn't have anything physically wrong with me.

I prayed about it with Cheryl, but I felt awkward talking to the Lord. I had not prayed regularly, and after months of virtually neglecting Him, I felt guilty asking Him to guide the surgeon.

Nevertheless, my prayers were answered, and I was euphoric when I woke up in the hospital room and there was no numbness in my leg or arm. The operation was a complete success. Although I wore a neck brace for six or seven weeks, I was able to walk. I wasn't able to work strenuously in the business for a long time, but we were making good money, and new business was coming in every day. During that period Cheryl and I went to Disneyland. One of the rides I wanted to take was the Pirates of the Caribbean.

''You can't go on that,'' Cheryl said.

''I'll be careful,'' I told Cheryl. ''I'll hold myself up so I won't feel any jarring.''

That ride I wanted to go on is a log ride. As we moved along the line to take the ride, we passed signs that told us to remove our eyeglasses before climbing into the hollowed-out metal log that floats in a water trough. There were other signs warning people with high blood pressure, pregnant women, and those with nervous disorders not to take the ride.

By that time we were near the ticket man at the gate. He saw my neck brace and wasn't sure he should let me get on the ride.

''Will you take responsibility?'' he asked.

''Yes,'' I said, and got into the log. The ride began, and the log was slowly moved to a higher and higher level within a water trough. Then it started down, jerking sharply to the left, then to the right, then dropping almost straight down.

Fortunately, I didn't get hurt, but it was another good example of my tendency to be reckless.

In the next few months, the pain from the operation disappeared. I had recovered fully and was able to work vigorously, and the business prospered. I became one of the directors of the Felton Business Association (FBA), and I worked hard to help make the town grow. Businesses began to move into the area, and there were other good developments. I started informal talks among the sheriff's department, police department, and the district attorney's office in an effort to stop the increase in crime that our community was experiencing. Eventually I became president of the FBA.

Then I joined the local chamber of commerce and became a director of community affairs. Incorporation of the community was discussed because we were being threatened with annexation by Scott's Valley and Santa Cruz; some land that adjoined Felton was being incorporated by those towns. In fact, the FBA started a committee to incorporate Felton. I was the public relations representative for the committee and served as a liaison between the incorporation committee and town officials who made the decision about the incorporation.

Although we never went through with the incorporation, people thought Felton would be incorporated, and they talked about who was going to be mayor and who was going to be the next councilman. My name was brought up many times, but I decided to ease out of politics and concentrate on my business.

Despite these successes, our finances had been clouded by the fact that the insurance company would not pay our hospital bills. We were paying premiums to an agent for a medical insurance policy, but when I made a claim for payment of the bills during my hospitalization for neck surgery, company officials told us they knew nothing about our policy. It had never been acted upon. Apparently, the agent had been pocketing the money.

The result was that our hospital bills were sent to credit companies that were demanding immediate payment. Our attorney advised us to file suit against the insurance company and pay a little on all our bills. As we followed that advice, the credit bureaus placed pressures on us. We sent out letters that the credit companies would be paid as soon as possible. In addition, we had several business-related bills.

Meanwhile, the insurance company fired our agent, and he declared personal bankruptcy. He was unable to keep his house because California law allows that when a person declares bankruptcy. That meant we did not have recourse to either the insurance company or the agent. Through the years and with God's help, however, we have been able to pay every dime.

5

The Best in the Area

Early one Friday morning, a maroon Cadillac pulled into a parking space in front of our shop, and a stocky, balding man and his blonde wife came in. I had been on my way out the door to deliver a piece of furniture, but they wanted an estimate.

They showed me a photograph of a Victorian table about 110 inches by 48 inches made of solid walnut. It had five legs with fancy spindle carvings and intricate marble inlay along the edges of each side. It had been made in Italy around 1870 or 1880.

"The Habers Furniture man said you were the best in the area, but expensive," the woman said. Her husband was a retired doctor, and she wore a big diamond ring.

"You've got the first part right," I said. "Now let's get on to the second part. I'm not expensive."

"I don't really care how much it costs," the man said. "I've got a houseful of expensive antiques that I would like refinished. I just want the best job possible."

There were scratches in the table top that had to be removed by taking about one-sixteenth of an inch off the surface. But the owners wanted to keep the wormhole effect of the original finish. That made the job extremely difficult, because sanding would remove the worm holes, and I would have to carve new ones. I usually did that by using a shotgun to shoot buckshot into the table from a safe distance and refining those holes with hand carving.

51

Years ago, before the fine finishing materials and preservative treatments now available, worms would get into many pieces of furniture. As a result, antiques often have worm holes. Beginning refinishers generally fill them with putty. Thus, legitimate antiques are given a whole new look. However, the proper way to treat wormholes is to fill them with oil to kill whatever is in them. That preserves the genuineness of the antique.

After some brief calculations, I told the doctor and his wife that I could do the job for $1,500. They agreed to the estimate. The work took more than a week, and creating those artificial worm holes really became tedious.

The couple were so happy with my work that they asked me to do more work for them. During the next few months, I refinished everything in their house. Their friends saw the way their refinished furniture looked and also wanted work done. Before long, I had so much business that I couldn't handle it all.

On an afternoon a few weeks later, a scientist asked me to come by his house to look at his oak piano. He wanted it refinished to look like rosewood. Oak is very porous. It usually is golden or white with small, lateral grains, or no grain at all. It's not as valuable to collectors as the decorative woods: rosewood, walnut, mahogany, and cherry. Rosewood is a rare wood. It's deep reddish with wide, black or deep brown, swirling grains.

It was a difficult job. He knew it and accepted my estimate of $5,600. I had to sand the grain out and then use woodfill to smooth over the pores of the oak. Large grains would have to be carved in and a black wood dye and redwood dye applied to make different tones. During the next few weeks, I often regretted taking the job because it required such tedious detail. But after many days I was finished, and the piano looked beautiful. Only an expert would be able to tell it wasn't rosewood.

Jobs like those helped our little shop become known as the best in the area for refinishing. In fact, a local newspaper published a whole column on the history of my family and the business. The columnist watched as I recarved the scrollwork on the antique frame of an original gold tapestry print showing George Washington in a garden in Virginia. The frame had been in a fire, and some of the carvings in it were broken off. I glued blocks of wood to the frame and carved grapes, leaves, and baskets of flowers so that it looked intact. The writer's article really boosted the business and spread our reputation for being a shop of quality and integrity.

Business was so good that we decided to move the store and shop to a small shopping mall next to the bank in downtown Felton, and Cheryl and I lived in a beautiful apartment above the business. That proximity to the bank enabled us to have coffee with bank employees at least once a day. Through these conversations they became familiar with us and our business. That helped, because there were times when I would write a check overdrawing our account by several thousand dollars, and the bank would cover it. The officers knew the cash flow was slow, but that we were doing a lot of business. They knew we were well-established in the community. They also cared about people and were willing to take some risks to help.

As the months went by, I reinjured my back several times while working, and the doctors could do very little for me except prescribe drugs to relieve the pain. The extensive medication caused my blood pressure to be high, and nerve damage had caused a bad case of psoriasis. By July 1973, the back pain and the psoriasis were making work and life miserable.

When I would wake up in the morning, it often felt as if needles were being stuck into the thoracic area (the middle part of my back, right behind the heart). To get up, I would roll out of bed onto my knees. After a few minutes I would try to straighten and stand up, but usually my legs became cramped, and I couldn't stand up. So I'd lie flat on my back to relax the muscles.

Sometimes as Cheryl and I would be lying in bed at night, she'd see the tension on my face and know that I was in pain. On occasion my leg would shake from muscle response to a pinched nerve.

I wanted to go to the Stanford Medical Center for my back and the severe case of psoriasis I had developed, but the costs were too high. I finally was able to get proper hospital insurance, but it carried a rider that said the company would cover any injury *except* my back because of the operation I had had in 1972. Because I am a veteran and didn't have to pay for treatment, I decided to enter the Veterans Administration hospital in Palo Alto during the summer of 1973.

After going through the admission process and being examined, I was placed in traction in a room with several other patients. Some were smoking marijuana and several were drinking, making it difficult to get any rest. I tossed and turned for hours before the ward settled down and I drifted off to sleep. I was exhausted and had fallen into a deep sleep when an older man woke me up by sitting on me and starting to get into my bed.

"Sir, this is the wrong bed," I said. "You can't get in this bed."

He acted as though he were drunk, but he heard me and changed his mind about getting in bed. He stood up clumsily and shuffled away, and I started to go back to sleep. Suddenly I heard the old man fumbling around my bed again. I looked up just as he urinated on me.

He collapsed on the bed, and I screamed for a nurse, falling out of bed and further damaging my back while trying to get away from him.

A nurse came running and tried to calm me down by giving me an injection. Then I called Cheryl and told her to call Bert Talcott, the U.S. Representative for our district.

When his secretary answered the phone the next day, Cheryl

explained that she was a constituent from Talcott's district and asked to have Talcott call her back.

Within an hour he returned Cheryl's call, and she told him everything. He was very reassuring. He promised to work on our case, and when Cheryl hung up, she was confident he would do something for us. In fact, Talcott must have called the hospital immediately, because Cheryl got a call at our shop. "Do you know what calling your congressman does?" the caller said. "Do you know you're lucky to get benefits?"

Later we learned that Talcott was on the veterans committee of the House of Representatives; therefore, a complaint by one of his constituents caused the VA problems.

Cheryl had dozens of conversations with Talcott. Every day for several weeks, either he or his secretary called me to see how I was progressing. Even after I got out of the hospital, he continued to call us.

Because of him I began to get the royal treatment. I was moved into a private room and received special attention. However, the first night that I slept in the private room, someone slashed a photograph of Cheryl that I had placed on my bedside table. The next morning, I saw the slashed picture and read the note that had been placed near it. "You better keep your mouth shut or you'll never get out of here alive," it said.

I had already talked, so I couldn't understand why someone would write me a note like that. But the anonymous note, placed at my bedside while I slept, terrified me. I called Talcott and told him what happened. Then I called Cheryl. "Get me out of here," I said. "They're going to kill me."

She asked the hospital for my release, but they told Cheryl that I couldn't leave for a month because they were going to do major surgery on my back and give me treatment for psoriasis. Then, surprisingly, early on a Friday morning, the hospital called Cheryl and told her to pick me up.

"What?" she said. "Yesterday you told me that he was

going to stay there a month, that he had to have surgery and was supposed to be getting special treatment.''

''No. Come and get him right now.''

I looked terrible, all red and sweaty. I obviously had a high fever, but they told Cheryl, ''Oh, no, he's fine. You can take him home.''

Cheryl arrived by midmorning, but because of administrative technicalities I was not released until late afternoon. By the time we reached Felton, I realized that my fever was worse than the doctors had led me to believe. Cheryl called the Veterans hospital. ''He's got a temperature of 104 or 105. He's burning up.''

The person on the other end said it was nothing serious. ''Just give him aspirins, and he'll be fine.''

But I got worse, and Cheryl called the hospital repeatedly for a prescription or any kind of medication stronger than aspirin. Later, when she tried to make the Veterans hospital pay the bills, they said she had never called. Fortunately, we had kept our phone bills, and she showed them the records of long-distance calls to the hospital.

When I woke up at about four o'clock Sunday morning my fever was worse, and my mouth was parched. I walked to the kitchen for a glass of water. I was so thirsty that I didn't even put on a robe. Because we were fairly new to the apartment, I moved cautiously. As I was groping in the semidarkness, my left knee buckled and I fell, hitting my head on the wooden end of a sofa arm. I hit the coffee table as I fell and made a terrible racket.

The noise startled Cheryl. She sat up in bed and reached for me, presumably sleeping beside her. Then she realized I had made all the racket, and she turned on the bedside lamp and rushed into the living room. There I was, sprawled in my underwear, unconscious on the floor. She felt my forehead, and it was burning with fever. She didn't know what was wrong, but she couldn't arouse me and my temperature was high, so she thought my condition was critical and called the rescue squad.

The fire department was nearby, and the rescue squad arrived quickly. They checked me out and decided that I should be in a hospital, but when I regained consciousness I started acting crazy. I was feverish and had been stunned by the fall. I couldn't think clearly. I kept lashing out and kicking at the firemen. Finally, they strapped me onto a stretcher and carried me down a narrow hallway and through a narrow door. Because the hallways were so narrow, the four men couldn't get me down the stairs without lifting me over the railing.

Cheryl told the firemen to take me to Community Hospital in Santa Cruz. I still owed bills at Dominican Hospital, and Cheryl was afraid I would not be admitted there. She also was unsure whether Dr. Magid and Dr. Scibetta would treat me because we owed them money for the surgery the year before. However, Dr. Scibetta drove to Community Hospital and examined me.

"Have him come over to my office tomorrow, and I'll look at him," he told Cheryl.

The next day, about an hour before the fire department took me to Dominican, I received a long-distance call from the VA hospital. A brigadier general in San Francisco told me he would take care of me personally. He wanted to send a helicopter to Santa Cruz to pick me up. A few minutes later I talked with Congressman Talcott, and he told me not to worry about the VA.

Unfortunately, when we got to Dominican, the business office would not admit me.

"Don't worry about it, Tom," one of the members of the rescue squad said. "We're going to call a friend." He called Pastor Arvid Carlson, the minister of the Felton Evangelical Free Church. Pastor Carlson was highly respected in the church and with the doctors. He called Dr. Scibetta and told him he would take full responsibility for all my bills. Then he came and visited me after I was admitted.

A member of Pastor Carlson's church and a customer of ours,

Mrs. Mary Anderson, learned about our predicament when she visited the hospital. She offered to loan us the money to pay the bill for Dominican and for Dr. Magid.

"Is she a relative?" Dr. Scibetta asked.

"No," Cheryl said.

"What's the matter?" Mrs. Anderson said as she came over to where we were. "She doesn't have any relatives. I'm her friend."

Two nurses were walking into the room when I opened my eyes the next morning. One took my temperature, and the other was writing on a clipboard. The nurses were not wearing masks or gowns as all visitors to my room had been, but they left before I was fully awake, and I didn't realize I was better.

Almost immediately after that, Dr. Petrelli walked in.

"How do you feel?" he asked.

"Real good," I said.

"I'm not sure what's happened," he said, "but whatever you had is in remission."

"Praise the Lord," I replied.

"During the night your condition seemed improved, and this morning you have no fever," he said.

"When am I going to get out, Doc?" I asked. "I've got a lot of work to do."

"It'll be another day at least," he replied.

I jumped out of bed and plopped down in a chair to talk to Cheryl on the phone. I was excited, and I was showing off a bit about how happy I was to be going home.

After the incident, Jim went home and called his brother John in Tucson. John had told Jim he would remember me at a prayer meeting. Later, at about two in the morning, John called Jim and told him that his prayer group had pleaded with God for me. He told Jim that he was confident I would recover.

The next day, Jim came to see me in the hospital and found me talking excitedly with Cheryl.

"What happened?" he asked.

"The doctor says I'm going to be all right," I said.

"When did they find out?"

"I guess they came in about two this morning."

My recovery was incredibly fast. Clearly, the Lord had been at work, and the tangible evidence that He knew about my problems and was at work in my life was humbling. I was bubbling with excitement because the Creator of the universe knew about me and my problems, and I had tangible evidence that He had worked in my life. I can't tell you how good that felt. It gave me a sense of confidence and acceptance that I had never known. I had been so lonely for so many years. I had been humiliated so many times during my teenage years that I really did not think much of myself. But now I felt I had worth. The God of the universe knew me and cared about me. I didn't have to impress Him or anybody else. I was accepted.

Dr. Petrelli saw me periodically. During each appointment, I talked to him about the Lord. He asked many questions because he was going through a great deal of stress from family problems.

Eventually his life changed remarkably, and more than four years later he stood up in a crowd after hearing me speak.

Oh-oh, I thought. *What's he going to say?*

"It's remarkable," he told the audience. "I know this man. He was a patient of mine. He was a nervous, broken shell of a man, but through the love of Jesus he's whole."

The audience broke into applause. Now Dr. Petrelli is an active Christian, conducting regular Bible studies at Dominican Hospital.

Meanwhile, we received medical bills from Dominican Hospital, but we didn't believe we should pay for them, because the only reason I had gone there was that I had not received help at the VA hospital. Congressman Talcott agreed with us, and he negotiated with the VA. After several weeks the VA assumed responsibility, and we were free of medical indebtedness for that hospital stay.

Shortly after my release from Dominican, I was rushed to the hospital again, this time to Community Hospital with severe chest pains and another fever. Dr. Scibetta ordered X rays of my lungs and saw symptoms of tuberculosis and began treatment. Because tuberculosis is contagious, I was placed in isolation. I was having problems breathing, and my temperature was very high.

Only family members who wore gowns and face masks were allowed to visit me. The doctors were not sure I had tuberculosis. It might be some rare disease that causes the breakdown of the blood cells, they said. They were really concerned because my lungs showed scar tissue, and they didn't know where the scarring came from. I was so weak I could hardly move, and my fever was getting worse. They couldn't find anything to treat it. Nothing was working, and Cheryl was distraught because the doctors showed increasing uncertainty about the diagnosis.

I was afraid. I didn't know what was wrong with me, and for the first time I thought it might be something serious—that I might be dying. I was so weak that I could hardly lift my head, and my fever was extremely high. In the past I had been hospitalized for back problems or psoriasis, but never for something as critical as this high fever. I felt that I was ready to die, but I hated to leave Cheryl. *Please, Lord, give me another chance,* I begged.

In desperation she called Jim Cojanis and asked him to get hold of Kenny Foreman, a local evangelist Jim had talked about many times.

Her phone call was based on an incident several weeks earlier. Cheryl and I had been watching television. Cheryl turned the dial and stopped on a channel that had a Christian program. She wasn't very interested in such things, but this show caught her attention. It featured Foreman's life story. He is a charismatic minister who claims to have been miraculously healed when he was a child. This was new to me and Cheryl, and we became fascinated by the program. I dialed Jim Cojanis's telephone number. "Quick, turn on channel 11," I said. "There's a program I want you to watch." Then I hung up. After it was finished, I called again. "What did you think of the program?" I asked. As the man on the other end of the line began to answer, I realized I was not talking to Jim. I had dialed the wrong number twice.

"I'm sorry," I apologized.

"That's all right. I needed that," the man said.

When I told Jim what had happened, he responded in a way I had not expected.

"You know, Tom, if God had wanted me to watch that program, I would have seen it. But God used you to bring this other person to see it."

Cheryl remembered this earlier incident and thought that Foreman, pastor of one of the largest churches in San Jose, might be able to help. We were desperate, just calling anyone and everyone who might be able to do something. We were looking for magic.

Jim asked to speak to Foreman, but he's a busy man. He has a large church, a television ministry, and many responsibilities. Jim explained that he had to talk to Foreman because he had a friend who was very sick. When Foreman heard that, he came to the phone and prayed with Jim. After praying for several minutes he told him, "I know Tom's going to be all right."

At that point an internist walked into the room with a nurse. And then, for some reason, I was suddenly firmly convinced that I would get well. Then I felt a strong breeze or wind come across the room, and I felt as if I were surrounded by a ball of light. I was so weak and dehydrated that I couldn't move, and a figure of a person appeared at the end of the room. I could only make out a shadow. It was so beautiful that at first I could only stare.

The light seemed to dim the whole room as television lights do when a camera crew is in action. My face projected that light.

Nobody else saw the light or figure, but Cheryl later told me that my eyes glowed, and she saw joy in my face. "You just sat up, Tom, with your hands outstretched, and then you said, 'Lord, thank You. Thank You. I know I'm going to be all right.' You laid back and looked over at me and you said, 'Everything's going to be all right now because God is taking care of me.' You just laid back and relaxed."

Later Jim called me back and told me he had talked to Foreman and that they had prayed for me and Foreman believed I would recover. They had prayed at about 7 p.m., Jim told me, and that had been when I saw the figure of light. That was comforting, because I realized I had come to a dead end. I felt compelled to commit everything to Jesus. That night I told Jim and Cheryl about the decision I had reached that afternoon.

"I know I've been saying I would devote my life to Christ, and something always seemed to come along to prevent it. But if God will just pull me out this time, I'll devote my life to Him. That's all there is to it."

Soon after that, I did begin to heal very rapidly. And even though I put off the commitment many days, it was a turning point that would eventually end in full-time Christian service.

The next afternoon, I felt someone watching me, and I looked through the door of my room into the hall, where a man and a woman were staring at me.

"Come on in," I called to them.

Apparently, they had heard about all the trauma I had experienced and came to the hospital to see me. They said they were having problems and wanted to hear my story. As they listened, they began to realize what the Lord could do. They had previously tried all sorts of therapy to snap out of their depression. We talked and prayed together, and later I learned that their visit was the beginning of their escape from depression.

When I left the hospital, Pastor Carlson and I continued the friendship started when he had first got me into the hospital, and I occasionally visited his church. He kept encouraging me to live up to my commitment to the Lord.

The doctor told me not to work anymore, not to do any lifting. I wasn't even able to carry a bag for Cheryl. I continued to work, but I increasingly spent time at home, reading the Bible and taking courses in psychology.

When I had first talked about it, Cheryl had objected to my being in the ministry. "You can't afford to now," she would say. "We've got too much responsibility with the business. That's all there is to it." But after the experience in the hospital room, she became supportive of the calling I felt.

Nevertheless, I really was weak after getting out of the hospital. I spent most of my time at home, recuperating.

6
Emergency Treatment

had felt an uneasiness all day, and by evening a vague nauseated feeling had come over me, a sense that everything was not all right. *It's just a case of the blahs,* I thought; *the rainy weather is depressing me.* I was lethargic and disgustingly irritable.

My uneasiness should have bothered Cheryl's mother, who was a guest in our home for several days during February 1974, but she was sympathetic toward me. She was taking care of the details of moving and settling affairs before going on to Hawaii, where Cheryl's dad had already started supervising construction of an industrial project. She saw me during the days when Cheryl was at work and muscle spasms prevented my pursuing normal activities, and she repeatedly offered encouragement. She realized the cause of my grumpiness.

But I knew I was bad company that day, so I decided to go to bed early. I wanted to sleep away whatever was bothering me. I must have been extremely tired, because I fell asleep right away and wasn't even roused when Cheryl came to bed. Several times during the night I almost awoke, however, tossing and turning with a recurring dream that would run almost to the end. Then I'd nearly awaken, and it would start again. Finally, I woke up feeling a gurgling in my stomach. I got up and took two antacid tablets from the medicine chest, poured myself a half glass of water, and swallowed the pills. I set the glass on the sink and turned on the hot water tap. I soaked a washcloth until it was steaming, gingerly squeezed the water out of it, and then held it against my face.

It's a technique I often used to relax. The hot cloth opened my pores and seemed to relax my face. I rinsed out the washcloth and hung it up, then grabbed a bath towel and briskly rubbed my face until it tingled. Finally I returned to bed.

But I still couldn't sleep. I lay on my back for five minutes, on my right side for a couple more, and then on my left side. Finally, I tried my stomach. Nothing worked. I just couldn't get comfortable, and my tossing and turning awakened Cheryl.

"What's wrong?" she asked.

"My back hurts, and I feel crampy in my stomach."

By this time Cheryl and I had been married about two years, and I had been in and out of the hospital so many times that she was beginning to doubt my complaints.

"It's just nerves," she said, rolled over, and drifted back to sleep.

I could hear the hum of the clock radio as the seconds dragged by, and I grew more nauseated. I eased out of the covers and went back to the bathroom. Without turning the light on, I lifted the toilet seat and vomited.

Now I'll feel better, I thought, hoping that the worst was past. But it wasn't. I went back to bed, and the ache in my stomach became a dull throb. Every few minutes a sharp jab took my breath away.

Lord, I can't take it, I prayed. *I'm tired of being sick.*

Cheryl heard my mumbling. "You're making it worse than it is," she said. "What do you want to do, run to the hospital?"

Those words hurt. She thought I was faking, that I really

didn't have physical pain. "Go ahead. Run. Run to the hospital," she said. "There's nothing wrong with you. Just make more bills that we can't pay."

She was angry and frustrated. She had married a big, healthy man who had become a helpless, whimpering figure with chronic ailments.

After many minutes I heard her heavy breathing, but my pain continued, and there was no sleep. I got up and placed a cold washcloth on my stomach. That seemed to help, so I went to the kitchen and placed several ice cubes on the washcloth, wrapped them up, and placed the cloth on my stomach. That eased the pain, but the nausea continued.

I don't know how I made it through the night. I must have dozed once and a while, but most of the night I lay with the cloth on my stomach, waiting for morning.

When Cheryl woke up and found me holding an ice pack to my stomach, she became angry. "You're not hurting. Quit acting like a baby," she shouted. She was frustrated. She knew psychosomatic medicine, and she found it difficult to believe anybody could be sick as often as I was. I always looked healthy, but deep down inside herself, she knew I loved her and wouldn't pretend. So she also felt guilty for yelling at me and going to sleep while I quietly tried to ease the pain and not interrupt her sleep. I think she was hoping I wouldn't feel pain if she told me there was no pain, but she knew better.

Cheryl's mother heard the shouting. She slipped into her robe and walked into the kitchen, where Cheryl was fixing sandwiches for her lunch and preparing breakfast.

"How can you talk that way to Tom?" she asked.

Cheryl showed no remorse. "He gets a little stomachache, and he wants to run to the hospital," she shouted. "If he'd just relax a little, he'd be okay."

She stormed out of the room to dress before leaving to open the store, and my mother-in-law stared in distress at me as I sat holding the ice pack to my stomach, my head hanging in shame.

It was a miserable morning, and when Cheryl returned at two that afternoon, she was just as angry as when she had left. She tossed the car keys on the table, looked at the refrigerator, then slammed the door. I know she had taken more than enough of my illnesses. She was letting me know that it was time for me to quit being sick, that I was trying her patience.

I felt sorry for myself. Tears slid down my cheeks as I lay quietly on the sofa in my robe with a warm quilt over my legs. I didn't want to be sick, and I didn't want to cause Cheryl problems. I knew I was pitiful.

Cheryl had come home to take her mother to dinner at the Brave Bull Restaurant in San Jose and then to the airport for a flight to Hawaii. I reluctantly kissed them good-bye, and they left.

But the throb in my abdomen continued. Finally I called Dr. Kenneth Reed, one of several doctors who took care of me. He was at home, but he said he'd meet me in the emergency room at Community Hospital in Santa Cruz.

I dressed carefully so I wouldn't aggravate my stomach and cautiously drove to the hospital. After a brief examination by Dr. Raymond Nelson, the doctor on duty who often cared for me, orderlies helped me take off my clothes and placed me on a tablelike cart. Then X rays were made.

The orderlies had rolled my cart into the hall by the time Dr. Nelson could evaluate the film. Only a few minutes had passed when he walked up to me and said, "Tom, we've got to operate immediately. You've got a ruptured appendix."

"Let me call my wife first," I said. There was a wall phone right beside the cart. Dr. Nelson saw that I didn't have my clothes, so he reached into his pocket, found a dime, and placed it in the telephone slot while handing me the receiver. I dialed information and got the number of the Brave Bull. Then I hung up, placed the dime in the slot, and charged the call to my home number.

"Brave Bull," someone said on the other end of the line.

"This is an emergency call," I said. "I'm trying to reach Mrs. Cheryl Scarinci. She's a blue-eyed, blonde woman in her mid-twenties. She's with her mother, and they're having dinner."

"Just a moment, please."

The next voice I heard was Cheryl's. "Tom, what is wrong with you? This has gone far enough. I'm eating—"

She was about to slam the phone down, but I interrupted her. "I'm in the hospital, Cheryl. I've got a ruptured appendix, and they're going to wheel me into surgery as soon as I hang up."

There was silence on the other end. Then, "Oh, my gosh. . . . Please forgive me, Tom. I'm sorry."

"That's all right, Cheryl. I just wanted you to know I'll probably be in surgery when you get back. I've got to go."

I gave the phone to the orderly, who placed it on the hook and started pushing my cart toward the operating room.

When Cheryl hung up the phone, she returned quickly to her table. Her face was ashen and her eyes shifted with guilt as she related my condition.

"Tom's always got something wrong with him," she said. "Can you believe a ruptured appendix?"

They talked quietly at their table for almost half an hour before driving to the airport, where Cheryl left her mother before returning to Santa Cruz.

My recovery was slow. Although I was only in the hospital a week before I was released, Dr. Nelson continued to treat the infection in my system. However, after several days, the surgical wound itself became infected, and my fever soared to 106 degrees.

Cheryl called Dr. Nelson, and he met us at his office and eased me up on his examining table.

"Cheryl, come over here," he said. He slid my shirt away from my abdomen. He knew Cheryl had studied medicine.

"Can you still handle these?" he asked as he gave her two clamps.

"Tom, it's going to hurt, but we've got to do it now," he said.

"You're not going to cut me open without putting me out or giving me something, are you?" I asked anxiously.

"We don't have time," he said, and placed a towel in my mouth. "Bite on this."

"Cheryl, hold this arm and start blotting as I make the incision."

Cheryl helped him as he cut open the stitches, and I screamed as he probed the sides of the wound and the pus oozed out.

"It's going to be OK," Cheryl said. "This is nothing like you've been through. You're going to be all right."

After about ten minutes of probing and blotting, Dr. Nelson put down his scalpel. "We're going to leave the wound open and let it drain," he said. He wrapped gauze loosely over it to absorb what came out.

Seeing the infected wound reminded Cheryl that she had prevented me from coming to the hospital earlier. Now I was suffering because of her attitude. "Honey, I'm sorry," she whispered as she quietly shook tears away. "I'm sorry I didn't believe you."

The dressing was changed every day for several weeks. Finally the infection was eliminated, but the ruptured appendix is a good illustration of the physical problems that seemed to be an integral part of my life. They seldom happened to others, and many people found it difficult to believe my situation.

During those years Cheryl was rarely ill. If health problems were going to happen to anybody, they seemed to happen to me. I hated it more than she did, but I couldn't get that across to her. Yet, she realized the pain I went through that day in Dr. Nelson's office.

"I'll never doubt you again," she said.

It was a generous expression of patience, but it still did not help to close the gap that had begun to exist between us. Cheryl and I no longer were as close as we had been before my many ailments. Part of the problem was my physical condition; during the five years between June 1972 and June 1977, I was seldom able to have physical relations with her because of the pain.

Also, Cheryl was frustrated by problems in the business. "You're too easy. You're a sucker," she used to say to me. "People take advantage of you."

That was the biggest problem we had. I didn't want to offend the customers. If a customer made a demand I would give him his way, even when I obviously was in the right.

Cheryl didn't like that. She thought I was letting people take advantage of me, and I think she also was frustrated because she knew it took a lot to give in, but that other people thought I wasn't much of a man because I did.

I tried to explain that it didn't matter what anybody thought, that my doing what I thought right was the important issue.

These tensions between Cheryl and me were intensified when her doctor told her she would not be able to have children. I realized that much of the difficulty was because of my illness. I wanted to counteract that by living up to my promise to provide Cheryl with a new home within five years after we were married, and we began to look for a house.

Meanwhile, I had agreed to do an estimate on a table and chair for a woman who owned a house on Laurel Drive. Her daughter had been divorced and suffered a nervous breakdown, and no one was living in the house. When I went to the house to do the estimate, the woman was cleaning it in order to sell it. She had bought it for her daughter and son-in-law, but with the breakup of the marriage, she saw no need to keep it.

I didn't know about her plans, of course. I had come to make an estimate. I looked at the lion-claw dining room table that was made of oak and at a chatham back chair. As we talked, the woman showed me some of her other antiques. I was particularly interested in an Italian slant-top desk made of sacharin wood and inlaid with either rosewood or walnut. I asked her what she was going to do with it.

"Sell it," she said. "I have to sell the house, and I want to get rid of most of this stuff."

"How much do you want for the house?" I asked.

"Forty thousand dollars."

"That's too much," I said. "I don't have that much money, but I'd buy it if I did."

We talked a bit, and she agreed to sell it to me for $35,000 and $5,000 down.

"Just wait here," I said. "I want my wife to see this place. Don't go."

I drove quickly to the shop. "Cheryl, come with me," I said after running in. "I've agreed to buy a house for $35,000, and I want you to see it. We've got to put down a down payment."

She was shocked, but she wanted a house, and she was grateful that I at least had come to get her before any money had changed hands. She also saw the potential of the house. It was big, 2500 square feet with two fireplaces, but we faced several difficulties in buying the house. First, it needed extensive renovation. It was full of dog and cat droppings, all the walls were painted chartreuse, and the carpeting was a mess.

Moreover, we were having financial difficulties. Because of the ups and downs in the cash flow of our business, and because of our medical bills, we were not able to get a veterans loan for which we had applied. Finally, my ever present back problems complicated my recuperation from the appendix operation.

Nevertheless, while still recovering from the operation, we drove to San Francisco to talk to the head of the veterans loan program. My back hurt so much that I walked stooped over like an old man with stomach pains, but we had to get the loan. The woman from the VA listened intently to my explanation and promptly granted us the loan. Her decision surprised us. Despite our belief that we could get a loan, we never thought it could be so fast. We knew the Lord had provided it.

We began work on the house. There were workers everywhere. Termite inspectors found thousands of termites. A new septic system was installed, and all sorts of repairs and renovations were begun. The house was in complete disarray.

At the same time the lease on our apartment was about to expire, and we asked the seller if she would let us rent the house for two months while the repairs were being done. We were delighted when she agreed, because the move would help us financially, even though the payments were more than three hundred dollars a month and the repair work was so extensive that costs were higher than we had projected.

The condition of the house was not suitable for good family life, and our decision to move before the house was finished was probably a mistake. Not one room in the house was livable. In fact, the bathrooms weren't even working, so there was no toilet or shower. Cheryl and I got on edge and fought a lot, and Cheryl cried every day. Finally we got to the point that we were fighting all the time.

We had to have some relief, and when Cheryl's parents invited us to visit them in Hawaii, we decided to go for two weeks during April while work continued on the house.

About seven-thirty or eight on our second night on the islands, Cheryl and I crowded into an elevator at one of the plush resort hotels. We were going to have dinner in the restaurant at the top of the hotel, overlooking Honolulu and the Pacific.

The elevator had just started when Cheryl squeezed my hand. "Honey, I feel dizzy," she whispered. "I think I'm going to pass out."

Before I could reply, her knees gave way and she collapsed on the floor before I could grab her. The other passengers pressed tightly against one another to give her room to breathe as I knelt over her.

In a few seconds we were at the top floor, and several men helped me carry her out of the elevator. We placed her gently on a cushioned bench just opposite the elevator doors. After a few moments she opened her eyes and gradually regained her composure, but her sickness did not pass. Throughout the trip she had spells of nausea, which we thought were just the result of a nervous stomach. Nonetheless, we spent the days relaxing on the beaches and touring the islands. By the time we boarded the plane for the return flight, we were in good spirits.

Meanwhile, several points had been added on the Veterans Administration loan. A point is a percentage of the total sale and is usually paid by the seller. In this case a point equalled $750. Because the seller had offered us such a good price for the house, she was reluctant to make the additional payments. We couldn't afford to pay the extra points, though, so we were perplexed. The seller also wanted to close the deal.

As we talked to the seller one day, she said she would be happy if she could just get the equivalent of one point. That reminded me of the Italian desk, and I told her I would buy it from her for $750. She wanted to sell all her furniture, and the desk didn't look like much, so she agreed to it. She was happy to get the $750, and we were happy to have the desk.

7
God, Where Are You?

Enough renovation had finally been done on the house for me to begin painting. I rented a spray gun and went to work. I wore no mask, just a pair of shorts and shoes and socks. I wasn't good at it, and I got paint all over the place. By the end of the day I was completely covered with paint. I took the spray gun back to the rental store and showered before supper, but I didn't feel well.

I checked my temperature, and it was 102 degrees. I thought it might be the flu; although Cheryl seemed to be better since she had collapsed on the elevator in Hawaii, she also had been nauseated for several days. As a result I suggested that we both go to see Dr. Reed in Boulder Creek. After a preliminary examination, he had me admitted to the hospital and examined Cheryl. My condition was diagnosed as an ulcer, and early indications were that Cheryl was pregnant. I was treated for several days and released.

In August, Cheryl's mother had flown in from Hawaii to have a hysterectomy. She planned to spend several weeks with us before going into the hospital and a couple of months recuperating after the surgery.

My medical condition steadily deteriorated during this period, and bills continued to accumulate. We had to pay for pain killers for my back problems and medicine for my psoriasis, which had become extremely bad. I went to a dermatologist, and he explained that psoriasis often develops in people who suffer nerve damage from extensive medical tests. Each time I went to the doctor it cost fifty dollars and nearly fifty dollars more for medication. After three visits, I realized I was not getting any relief.

"Even if we hate the Veterans hospital," I told Cheryl, "at least I can get treatment at no cost."

"No," she said. "You're not going into the Veterans hospital. They'll kill you for sure this time."

I shared her anxiety. I didn't want to go to the VA hospital either, but my back condition had deteriorated and the itching and psoriasis was driving me crazy. I entered the VA hospital again.

I had hoped that a whole new record would be worked up on me, but the doctors checked my medical records and told me it looked as though I had hypertension and could have a heart problem.

"It's not a heart problem," I kept telling them. "It's my back."

"No, it can't be," the doctors said.

They wanted to take some tests before they attempted any surgery on my back. After a treadmill test, they said they had located some heart problems and asked for permission to do blood pressure tests and try a new treatment for the psoriasis.

Cheryl and I discussed the doctors' request and decided to go through with the tests, including a venogram. They said it wasn't dangerous, because it only involved the injection of dye into my bloodstream. I said OK and admitted myself to the hospital. The next morning they took me downstairs for a venogram.

The doctor started the injection slowly. "You're going to feel a hot flash," he said. "At that point you'll feel real sick to your stomach. Then you'll be OK."

I had just felt the heat flash in my face when he paused and said to his technician, "I've got to finish up a patient in the other room. Hold this syringe until I get back."

I thought he'd be back in a minute or two. But we waited and waited and waited. The technician was an attractive brunette in her mid-twenties, and we exchanged a few pleasantries as we waited for the doctor to return. After about twenty minutes, she grew tired of waiting and began to inject the dye.

Suddenly I felt as if I was burning up. My face was completely disfigured, and everything seemed foggy.

"Oh, no, I blew it," she said. "Doctor, help!"

A doctor came running. "What's going on?" he shouted. "Where's the oxygen? We're losing this guy."

There was no oxygen in the room, and an orderly ran into the room with oxygen and other paraphernalia.

Then I heard people yelling, "Stat, stat, stat." More doctors rushed in. Someone uncovered my chest, and someone else reached down and placed two round disks on my chest.

I felt a jolt that seemed to rip my chest. I was gasping for air, and I knew I was dying.

"We've got him," the doctor yelled.

I felt an injection into my chest and heard more shouting. The language was profane. I was going into cardiac arrest, and the doctors were fighting for my life. My heart hadn't stopped, but it was in fibrillation, the stage before cardiac arrest when the heart beats erratically—fast and then slow. Fortunately, they were able to restore a stable heartbeat.

I had suffered an allergic reaction to the dye, cutting off my oxygen. Eventually I was wheeled back to my ward, but nobody called Cheryl. She didn't even know what had happened until she came to the hospital at about eight that night. She saw all the spots on my face and a syringe of epinephrine taped to my bed and suspected that I had experienced a reaction to the dye. Epinephrine is like adrenalin in that it stimulates the heart when it goes into fibrillation. She walked out of the room to ask the head nurse what had happened. The head nurse wasn't at her station, so Cheryl stormed back to my room.

"Call Dr. Reed. He needs to know about this," she fumed,

picking up the phone and dialing his number. She handed me the phone, and I explained my situation to him.

"Sign out and come to Community Hospital," he told me. "I'll take the responsibility. You tell them you've got to get over here immediately."

We told the VA doctors what Dr. Reed had said, but they would not release me. In fact, they convinced me that I needed more tests. After undergoing a battery of tests, they found that my heart was in good condition.

A new diagnosis was needed, and a second-year medical student thought he had the correct one.

"It's a psychiatric problem," he said.

Maybe it is all psychological, I thought. *I had surgery in 1972. Everything should be all right.* I was very upset nonetheless. I had thought I had something wrong with me medically, and now a medical student was telling me my problem was psychological. He even called Cheryl and asked her to go to a psychiatrist. "I can't get off work," she told him.

That only intensified his interest and convinced him that Cheryl was afraid to face the "fact" that she had made me work too hard. The medical student told me Cheryl didn't love me and that all she wanted from me was a nice house and fine clothes.

I didn't need to hear that. For months I had felt guilty about the ailments that had kept me from working regularly, and after several days of harassment, I called Cheryl. "They are driving me crazy," I said. "They're beginning to make me think that I'm crazy, that you're crazy, and that your mother is crazy. And I know that everybody's crazy here."

Repeatedly the medical student explained that all this had happened because Cheryl forced me to work. He said she was an authority figure for me, and that I did not feel like I was being a good husband. I didn't believe him, but his words were confirming my worst fears—Cheryl eventually was going to leave me.

When I had had enough of the medical student, I phoned Dr.

Reed, and he told me to sign out. Cheryl was very pregnant and also working in the business, so she couldn't pick me up. However, my mother-in-law, who was not well herself, was willing to drive to Palo Alto to take me to Community Hospital in Santa Cruz.

"I'm going to leave," I told the medical student at the VA hospital.

"You can't do that," he said. "If you do, you'll die. You won't make it to Santa Cruz."

I knew he was trying to scare me, but it worked anyway. I was terrified. "I don't want to go to another hospital," I told my mother-in-law when she arrived. "I'm afraid this is going to continue."

I was afraid that, because of all the pain and suffering I was going through, Cheryl didn't love me and wasn't going to stay with me. "She doesn't love me," I told my mother-in-law. "She's been through too much pressure. Please don't take me down to Community Hospital. I'm afraid I'm going to lose her."

"Tom, she loves you," she kept saying to me. "She was just upset. Don't worry about it. She loves you. You're going to be OK. We love you." She finally talked me into checking out and leaving with her.

I still couldn't think logically, however, and I tried to make my mother-in-law turn off and go home instead of to the hospital. In the process, I worked myself into hysterics. I felt I couldn't breathe, and my chest seemed to be crushing my lungs. I started gasping for air.

"I can't breathe, Mom. I can't breathe," I gasped.

She quickly pulled to the side of the road. "What do I do?" she asked.

"Get me to the hospital," I said.

I blacked out, and she took off. She told me she went through stop signs and red lights, driving to save every second. She was afraid I would die before we reached the hospital.

She pulled into the entrance, stopped, and ran inside. She was ashen and breathless as she shouted, ''My son-in-law is having a heart attack! Please hurry!'' I was still unconscious when orderlies rushed out of the hospital with the cart. They started heart massage and immediately called Dr. Reed. He came and put a heart monitor on me and did electrocardiograms. He said it showed some forms of fibrillation, and I was moved into the coronary intensive care unit. I stayed there for several days, and only Cheryl and my mother-in-law could see me, and then only for a few minutes at a time.

Eventually Dr. Robert Finnegan diagnosed my ''heart problem'' as being disks in my back that were pinching a nerve and causing chest pains and shortness of breath.

With my being in the hospital so much, business was quite a burden for us, particularly Cheryl. She really wanted to please the customers but often found it impossible. That forced her to grow in her interaction with people. She was running the business much of the time and often had to explain why work wasn't done. She had to keep the employees happy, and she had to keep the books and do all the paperwork. As someone who had not previously been part of the job, Cheryl found running things to be a daily trauma. It was a new experience for her. She was a hard worker and very determined, but running the business was difficult, particularly during her pregnancy, when she was so sick.

Moreover, we didn't have many friends our own age. I had been sick for so long that most of our younger friends had left us. They had rallied around us in 1972 when I first got sick, but I had not been well for more than two years, and my friends never knew how I'd feel. We never could plan on having anybody to our house. If we ever did go anywhere or do anything, I usually felt a lot of pain, and people didn't like to see that. People just don't find it fun to be around those who are sick. When I first had health problems, many of our friends would help Cheryl with errands and little jobs around the house. But as my illnesses continued, other people had their own washers to fix, gutters to clean, cars to repair, and so on. Because of this, Cheryl had to do absolutely everything. She changed tires on the car and fixed things around the house in addition to taking care of the business.

Another result was that she and I were alone a lot, and I felt that because of me Cheryl was not having as full a life as she deserved. That made our situation even more tense. I felt guilty, but I also resented her because just seeing her reminded me of my guilt. Moreover, I felt so helpless because she had to leave her own career in July 1972 to run the business, and she had not been able to resume that career because I was sick so much.

In September, Cheryl's mother entered the hospital for a hysterectomy, but it was delayed several times. One afternoon, as I was looking at her medical records, I saw a note from her doctor that he wouldn't operate unless she quit smoking. I asked him about it, and he expressed concern about a possible respiratory problem during surgery.

"How do you think we can stop her from doing it?" her doctor asked me. "We just can't operate until she quits."

"I'll do what I can," I said, and walked back to Mrs. Friesen's room.

"Mom, what are you trying to do, kill yourself?" I asked. "We care about you. We love you." I explained to her that her condition was desperate. I took her cigarettes away from her and wouldn't let her smoke. Later I learned that she was asking people in the hospital for their cigarettes, but my efforts were putting limits on her smoking. She wasn't smoking two and a half to three packs a day as she had been, and the reduction helped.

Meanwhile, Cheryl was not having an easy pregnancy. One Friday in September, she had such severe dizzy spells that she went to her doctor in Watsonville, but he was delivering a baby and couldn't see her. She came home and had a terrible weekend. On Monday she went to see him again, and he found that her blood pressure was way up, so she was admitted to the hospital. More tests were performed, and they showed that Cheryl might have toxemia.

That diagnosis only intensified my fear of losing her, and I made the twenty-five mile trip south along the coast to Watsonville twice a day to visit her. I'd also drive the forty miles each day to San José to visit her mother. I'd go to the shop at about seven each morning to get paperwork done and set up jobs for the five employees who worked in the shop. Then I'd leave at about ten and drive south to Watsonville. Cheryl and I would visit for about an hour, and I'd return to the shop a little after noon.

At about half past two I'd leave the shop again for Alexian Brothers Hospital in San Jose, north and west across the Santa Cruz Mountains on Highway 17. I'd visit with Cheryl's mother and talk to her doctors. Usually she wanted to know about Cheryl. Because Cheryl was no longer visiting her she knew something was wrong, and I had to explain a little bit about Cheryl's condition. I was concerned, but I didn't want Mrs. Friesen to know it. Then, about half past four or five, I'd return to the shop and work until around six.

I'd have a hamburger or a sandwich for supper, a quick shower, and then I'd leave for Watsonville to visit Cheryl again. We would talk for about two hours before I returned home and went to bed about eleven. Sometimes I had to go back to work to get a job done, however. On those nights I didn't get to bed until one or two in the morning. This went on for a week, and the routine was beginning to get the best of me. And each day I realized more clearly that I couldn't live without Cheryl. She was very sick, and her blood pressure was extremely high. I didn't want her to become anxious about me for fear her condition would get worse, so I tried to endure quietly. But each day was almost impossible.

Moreover, I was concerned about the baby. I knew it would take Cheryl's attention from me, and that made me jealous and angry. I needed Cheryl so much that at that point there was no room for anyone else.

Fear and despair haunted me night and day, and the longer Cheryl was hospitalized the more frenzied I became. One afternoon after visiting her in Watsonville, I was returning to the shop along Highway 9. It is a beautiful, curving, blacktop highway through the redwood trees, but I didn't see any of the beauty. I was lost in my problems. As I rounded a sharp bend, I saw a place in the road where a nurse had lost control of her automobile and driven off the road. She plunged several hundred feet into a ravine. *How easy that would be,* I thought, and steered for the embankment. I really didn't want to die, though, and I came to my senses in time, jamming on the brakes and screeching to a halt.

There may have been a foot left before the truck would have plunged into the ravine, but I couldn't tell it. All I could see was the tops of the redwood trees that were growing from more than a hundred feet down the steep incline. I looked out through the windshield and sensed that I had stopped on the edge of eternity. My hands and shoulders trembled uncontrollably, like those of an addict who needs a fix or a child who has been swimming so long that his whole body shudders and his teeth chatter with cold. In a moment I knew I was capable of destroying myself, and I felt deep terror.

I felt as if in a dream in which I would stand on a high building and would not be able to avoid falling. The stark fear of realizing that I might not be able to keep myself from self-destruction dominated my consciousness, and I put the truck in reverse and backed slowly onto the highway. My heart was pounding so hard that I could feel it in my neck and I cautiously drove to the entrance of Henry Cowell State Park and turned in. I pulled into a parking area, slammed on the brake pedal, flung open the door, and started running. I ran as fast as my legs would carry me, totally possessed with panic. I had a feeling as if a giant blanket were being thrown down on top of me and I was running to escape before it fell and smothered me. Life was more than I could cope with alone, and I was sure I was losing my wife. I dropped to my knees when I reached the shade trees near the bank of the San Lorenz River, and, gasping for breath, I shouted at God.

"How am I going to take care of my family?" I said. I felt that Cheryl was in the hospital because of my problem. "God, where are You?" I yelled. "I don't feel like a human being anymore. Everything is going wrong. Why, why do I have to go on? Why do I have to keep suffering all the time?"

I kept asking Him if I could have some relief. I had no one to turn to. Cheryl didn't know me. I couldn't tell her how I felt. No one understood me. "Is all this problem imaginary?" I asked the Lord. "Is it real? Is it psychosomatic? Please, God, You've got to help me," I pleaded with a heaviness that oppressed me as I knelt under the big oaks and redwoods.

I must have been there two or three hours. When I was drained of all the emotional energy, I felt some relief, but the nauseating dread was still there as I walked slowly back to the pickup and drove north to the shop in Felton.

I was too exhausted to go to San Jose to see Cheryl's mother that afternoon, but I did drive back to visit Cheryl in the evening. "Why are you so late?" she asked.

"I had a lot of work to do," I explained, but I could tell she sensed something was not right. I didn't offer any further explanation, and she dropped the subject. Somehow I made it through Cheryl's days in the hospital without another incident as terrifying as that afternoon.

Even after she returned home and waited for the birth of our child, Cheryl still was not well. I felt heavy responsibilities, and I wasn't sure I was up to them. Then one night my back pain was extremely intense, and I got out of bed to take some pain-killing pills. After about a half hour, I got up and took a few more. Still no relief. I wanted to take a handful more. I got up, walked to the bathroom, and looked at the bottle. I knew what I was doing and rejected the idea.

I walked slowly back to bed, lay down, and began to cry.

"What's wrong, honey?" Cheryl asked.

"Oh, my back, Cheryl. It's just killing me, and the pills aren't doing anything."

As we talked, Cheryl learned that I had experienced an overwhelming urge to take a handful of pills and end the pain forever.

"That's OK, Tom," she said. "You didn't do it. You rejected the idea and you are just depressed at the thought of what you almost did. In the morning, you'll feel better."

"No, Cheryl," I said. "It's happened before." Then I told her about the urge to drive off Highway 9 and kill myself that afternoon when she was in the hospital.

Cheryl listened quietly. She realized how seriously pain had affected my mind, and we talked for several hours. Neither of us slept much, and most of the night I sat on the edge of the bed while Cheryl, more than eight months pregnant, tried to help me come to grips with myself. I confessed my dependency on her, my jealousy of the baby, and my total sense of failure.

I told her everything. I hadn't wanted to. I had thought it would scare her too much, but she knew that I was upset, and I believe our conversation that night helped me to make it through the next few months.

Cheryl always knew when I was going to end up in the hospital. Now she knew by the way I was acting that it was coming to that point. "I know what's going to happen," she said. "Before long you'll be in the hospital."

Sometimes she said that out of anger and frustration, but this night she understood. From then on she would watch me carefully. Everything I did, every pill I took, would be under her scrutiny, but at the same time she intensified her supportiveness. Now I didn't have to hide anything from her. I knew she was behind me more than ever.

8

Intruders in the Dark

Recovery came slowly for Cheryl's mother after her operation, but as the weeks passed she regained her strength. She helped with some of the tasks around the house and bought items for the baby because Cheryl continued to have problems. She was sick much of the time, and her mother's efforts to help often were an irritant. Both women were on edge.

The friction became almost unbearable. The baby was due the first week of December, but Christmas came and went; New Year's Day passed, and still the baby was not born.

"What kind of doctor do you have?" Cheryl's mother asked. "Doctors must not know anything these days. My doctor would not have let me go on this long. He would have induced labor."

Mrs. Friesen was not meaning to make things worse for Cheryl. She was deeply concerned; she couldn't understand how a woman could be more than six weeks overdue and the doctor wouldn't induce labor. But her anxiety only added to her daughter's worries. Cheryl also wondered why the baby had not arrived. Maybe her mother was right. Maybe her doctor didn't know what he was doing. After all, within a month after she had been told it would be impossible for her to have children, she was passing out in an elevator with symptoms of pregnancy.

We learned that Mr. Friesen was flying in from Hawaii for a hernia operation. He arrived on Friday, January 17, 1975, and on Saturday he and Cheryl's mother drove to Santa Rosa, in the San Francisco area, to visit Cheryl's brother Jack for the weekend.

That evening Cheryl and I had dinner at Dr. George Gibson's home in Boulder Creek, a home overlooking the lush fairways and greens of the Boulder Creek Country Club. Dr. Gibson was an administrator at San Francisco State University. He and his wife were customers of ours who had become close friends, and I often went to his house to play cribbage.

That night was particularly pleasant, and as the evening wore on, one of the guests casually predicted that the focus of much of our anxiety would soon be passed. "You're going to have your baby tomorrow," she said.

"How could that be?" Cheryl said, laughing it off. She hoped it would be true, but she had waited so long, and there were still no signs. We had reached the point that we wondered whether we really were going to have a normal, healthy child. We could hardly take the woman's quiet assurances seriously.

The next morning, January 19, 1975, the sky was a bright, deep blue, a gorgeous Sunday, and Cheryl and I decided to spend the day together, walking on the beach and relaxing. We had not had a day by ourselves in several months.

Before we had even eaten breakfast, however, Cheryl's water broke. "I think we'd better go to the hospital, because it's a long ride," I said.

"I'm not going to the hospital yet," she said. "When you go to the hospital you have to pay by the hour. I'm not going to sit there hour after hour just because my water broke."

I was terribly anxious. We had worked together on her

breathing and other aspects of natural childbirth, and I was worried about the details. I called the doctor but he wasn't in, and a nurse advised us to go to the hospital. That didn't mean anything to Cheryl. She was convinced she wasn't ready. She ashed her hair and shaved her legs. Meanwhile, I paced the floor and made more phone calls. I called Cheryl's parents, but they were out. I called the Gibsons and some of our other friends, but they were all out. Finally, we got in the car, and I drove nervously along the coast highway to Watsonville.

We were nervous as we went to the labor room. Cheryl had been so sick while she was pregnant that we were anything but calm as we waited. Then the contractions started. I counted and reminded her of the proper way to breathe.

Every fifteen or twenty minutes a nurse came in. "Oh, we've got a while to go yet," she said. "You're only about a third or fourth dilation. I'll call the doctor in a little while."

She had just left the room one time when Cheryl said, "Tom, I can't help it. I've got to push. I've got to push."

"Cheryl, it can't be yet. You shouldn't be pushing until the baby's almost there. Breathe deeply and calm down. Just hold back."

"I can't help it. Please don't leave the room."

"You can't push yet. You've got a long way to go."

I tried to call the nurse, but she wouldn't come in. I took a look, and sure enough, the baby's head was sticking out.

"She's having the baby," I said to the nurse after running to find her. "You better get in here right now."

The nurse came running into the room and took a look. "Oh, my word," she said, and rolled Cheryl into the delivery room. The doctor on duty was summoned, and he had begun to deliver Heath when our doctor arrived. Our doctor completed the delivery, and our beautiful little son came into the world.

After the delivery, I learned that Cheryl's parents had arrived at the hospital from Santa Rosa. I told Cheryl they were waiting to see her. Fifteen minutes after the birth, she took Heath in her arms, and I held her orange juice as we walked out of the delivery room and down the hall together. Cheryl's mother had been skeptical of natural childbirth, and Cheryl was determined to show her it worked. I gave Cheryl's mother the orange juice, but she was so unnerved that she dropped it to the floor.

"Cheryl, you're crazy to be walking around like that," she said. "You should be in bed."

Cheryl would have gone home that day, but because of her difficult pregnancy, and her female medical history, the doctor urged her to undergo a partial hysterectomy. He scheduled surgery, and she was in the hospital a week.

Meanwhile, Cheryl's brother and his girlfriend arrived in town. It was a full house when I brought Cheryl and Heath home, and it was chaotic. Cheryl's mother still could not do much work because she was recovering from her surgery, and the others were new to the house. I had to clean, fix meals, wash all the diapers, take care of Heath, and run the store.

It was more than we could take. Both Cheryl and I desperately needed peace and quiet. We were physically and emotionally drained. Each day seemed to be a struggle to survive while others made extensive demands on us. After a couple of days, Cheryl's brother and girlfriend left, easing some of the overcrowdedness.

Meanwhile, I tried to get life insurance because I had a new son, and I was worried that my estate might not be able to provide for him if I should die. The insurance company took my application and reviewed my health record before telling me that, because of my heart condition, I couldn't get a policy. "I don't have a heart condition," I said. "It's my back. I've never had a heart condition." I went to Dominican Hospital in Santa Cruz, walked the treadmill, and had my heart thoroughly checked. Dr. Robert Finnegan, a heart specialist, said I was fine. Finally the company said I could have risk life insurance, and we bought a policy.

After several weeks, Mrs. Friesen had regained her strength enough to do housekeeping, so she and Cheryl's dad rented an apartment while he had a hernia operation and went through a convalescent period.

By this time Cheryl was working a half day at the shop. As she regained her strength she lengthened her workday, and by the time Heath was five or six weeks old, we put a crib and a jump swing in a room about six feet by six feet, and Heath slept and entertained himself all day long. He was a good child. He loved being at the shop, and he seldom cried.

As he grew older we brought some toys to the shop, and Heath would play in the back office with his toys and the carpet samples. When he got tired, Cheryl would push together two gold chairs that were in the shop window, and Heath would sleep on them. He spent his first three years in that shop. It was his nursery, and amid customers' complaints and all sorts of concerns about my health, Heath was a reminder of God's graciousness. His sweet disposition often helped us to forget the problems of the business.

Cheryl's mother bought him a red lunch box with a Snoopy decal on the side. Cheryl would pack his lunch, and Heath would say he was ready ''to go to my work.'' Some days Cheryl would have to go back to the shop at night to catch up on paperwork, and Heath would stay home with me. I can't begin to tell you how useless that made me feel. I couldn't even do the paperwork. Instead I spent many days flat on my back on the floor of our living room. I couldn't read. I couldn't move. When the pain was not so intense I would work, but the off-days were more frequent than the work days. Most of the time, life was going on around me.

Fortunately, the business began to expand after the recession of 1974. Our little shop was doing great, but I had a feeling of despair and doom. I told Cheryl about some of my feelings as we were out driving one afternoon.

"What?" she said. "Everything's going great."

But my feelings were genuine.

The next morning I made a call in Santa Cruz to pick up furniture for a large upholstery and refinishing job. I had talked to the woman of the house when the order was placed, but I had no idea how beautiful her house was. I drove through a big iron gate and up a curving driveway to a big, Spanish-style mansion with a tiled roof and two expensive cars parked in the drive. I entered a spacious entry hall and saw high ceilings, arched doorways, and rooms decorated with all sorts of antiques, Persian rugs, and original art. I explained to the woman that I needed $500 down before I picked up the furniture. She walked into another room to get her checkbook, and while she was gone I overheard a conversation in the hallway in which two people were discussing a "drop" at Moss Landing, a remote area near Santa Cruz.

I recalled those words a few minutes later when she came back with a strongbox and paid me cash. *Oh, oh,* I thought as I looked at the strongbox. *He's into something big.* I took the money nervously, and several large, tough-looking men helped me load the furniture into my van.

Then I quickly drove back to the shop. Later I went to the district attorney's office and told him what I had heard, and that night I got two threatening calls from the same person. "You'd better forget anything you heard or saw in that house," the caller said.

When I finished the upholstery work a week or two later, I returned the furniture and gave the woman the bill for $2,000 but she told me she didn't have the money. I had to leave without any payment.

I'm the kind of person who would just as soon forget a debt, but Cheryl didn't care who it was. Two thousand dollars was a lot of money, and she expected to collect. She sent me several times for payment, but I never found the couple home. I would sit outside for hours, waiting for them, but they were never there.

I was just waiting for them to come home. It seemed the natural thing to do. I didn't realize how dangerous it was. After another threatening call, I talked to the FBI and learned that the police and FBI were also watching the house. "What's going on?" I asked.

"We'll have to level with you, Tom. You're really involved with dynamite," the FBI said. "Your life could be in danger if we put a tap on your phone. The guy skipped bail of $100,000. We don't know where he is, but he's a heavy dealer in drug traffic. The DA's office should have told you what was going on when you came in here."

Later, several FBI men came to my house, and I told them about overhearing a conversation concerning a big delivery at Moss Landing. The details led to a big raid.

I really must have been naive to continue to pursue payment. Also, Cheryl was insistent that whatever else the fellow did was his business; we merely wanted to collect for our work. So, just before the big raid, I drove to their house and asked for them.

"Never heard of them," a gardener said.

Obviously, I wasn't getting anywhere. I walked back to my truck and got in. Before I could start the engine and move out of my parking place, two large men sauntered up to my truck.

"What do you want with him?" they asked.

"He owes me money."

"You forget that money and get out of here. Make believe you never heard anything, or you'll find yourself sitting at the bottom of the ocean."

"Nobody is going to trick me," I said.

"I'm telling you, you better do what I tell you, or you won't live to find out."

One of them, a massive, burly-chested black man, pulled back his jacket, and I could see a gun in a shoulder holster. I didn't know who they were, but I remembered the burly men who helped me load the furniture, and I got the message.

By the time I got to the shop I was frightened enough to call the FBI and report the incident. But I just "forgot" about trying to collect the money.

I didn't think much more about the incident until a couple of weeks later. It was mid-September, and I was driving a van full of furniture on Highway 9 toward Santa Cruz. It's a mountainous, curvy road lined with tall trees. It's the road our shop is on, and I knew it by heart. Suddenly a blue pickup came shooting out of the entrance to Henry Cowell State Park. I tried to avoid a collision, but it hit me broadside, sending my van sideways down an embankment and against a tree. Furniture came down on top of me, but I had the presence of mind to look back at the highway. I turned and saw the truck leaving the scene, but I couldn't see the license plate. I thought I'd be all right if I could just get out from under all that furniture, but I was dizzy and couldn't get free. Finally the highway patrol arrived, helped me out, and took me to the hospital.

I had suffered a concussion and was experiencing severe pain in my lower back. The doctors wanted to do a myelogram but couldn't because I was allergic to the dye, and any more myelograms would have been dangerous.

During the two weeks I was in the hospital, I was in great pain in the lower back. It was the kind of pain you feel when the Novocain is not strong enough and the dentist hits a nerve in a tooth—only multiplied a hundred times. All I could do was lie still. However, the condition itself causes twitching. So I would move, and that would set off the pain again. Day after day the pain was so intense that I never knew whether I could make it another minute. Week after week the pain continued, convincing me that I had no hope. Without regular injections of morphine, I couldn't have made it. I was deeply depressed, afraid I would never be free of pain.

Meanwhile, I phoned Dr. and Mrs. Chester Laubscher, a Christian couple who had become customers of ours. We had refinished some of their antiques. In fact, they redecorated their house and asked us to reupholster their sofa and chair in a soft powder blue. They had appreciated the work, and we became good friends. Dr. Laubscher or his wife often dropped in at the shop, and we often visited in each other's homes. They lived in a three-story redwood house overlooking Monterey Bay. Huge windows and a deck went around the entire house, and, standing by the window at night, one could see the lights of houses and businesses twinkling in the distance below.

When I called, I told them I had been in an accident. They visited me several times, and Cheryl took Heath to their house before coming to visit me.

Unfortunately, Cheryl was badly hurt when the Rev. Joe Kennedy, an Episcopal priest, did not visit me once during the two-week hospitalization. I had met Joe when he walked into our shop one afternoon and asked to buy some carpeting for his house. He was a boisterous, ruddy-faced, six-foot, two hundred pounder a few years older than me with long, dark, wavy hair and soft, compassionate eyes.

We had talked for quite some time that day in the shop. His combination of ruggedness and warmth attracted me, and when he left he invited me to visit him in Ben Loman. I did several days later, and we became good friends. We often played golf together at the Boulder Creek Country Club, and Cheryl and I attended his church quite regularly. I was drawn to the Episcopal church by Joe's friendship. The church was close enough to my Catholic background and traditions to allow me to feel comfortable, and I could be involved because of my friendship with Joe.

I, too, was surprised that he didn't visit me in the hospital. We had become extremely close friends. I had been in the labor room with his wife when Joe could not be there, and we had shared many accomplishments and disappointments.

I had loved my participation with Joe in the ministry of the church of which he was a rector. I had worked on projects with him, and we had studied the Bible and prayed together many times about problems in the ministry. I had often thought about going to an Episcopal seminary, but during those fourteen days I made the decision to go, and as I lay on my hospital bed I wanted to talk to him about going to seminary. I had actually made a commitment in 1973, but it had been financially impossible, and I was too sick to go to school.

I was under Dr. Field's care constantly, and he had me exercising, swimming, and losing weight. He believed that exercise could relieve the disk problem in the thoracic area of my back. Moreover, he kept me on strong medication to relieve the pain, and I also took forms of codeine to try to get through the day. My back problems really hurt the business because I couldn't be at the store, and employees were taking supplies and not working to capacity. Because of all that, I sometimes went to work under great pain, figuring I had to. Eventually this intensified my problems. Every couple of weeks I'd be back in the hospital again for another week. The doctors couldn't do any surgery at that point because they couldn't do a venogram or myelogram to locate the problem.

Meanwhile, for some reason—maybe because of my feelings of inadequacy or because of guilt—I decided to buy a large plot of land in a rural setting and build the dream house I had promised Cheryl when we were married. It was November 1975, and land prices were beginning to increase rapidly in our part of California. On one of my land-viewing excursions, I saw a sign saying land was for sale by one of our customers who was a good friend. I went to his house (which was nearby), and he showed me a two-acre site that he would sell for $20,000. After some negotiation, he accepted a small down payment for the graded lot and a water share.

That was a lot of money in November 1975, but now you can't even buy a garden plot for $20,000. Real estate prices in the Santa Cruz area have skyrocketed since it became an oceanside bedroom community for San Jose, which is over the mountains and northeast of Santa Cruz. We figured we could make $40,000 profit on our house and build the kind of house we had always wanted.

We made these plans under conditions of extreme duress. My back was causing me continual problems, and I had been told not to work, not to do any lifting. Cheryl couldn't run the shop all by herself, however, so I continued to work whenever I could.

As the holidays approached, I began to think of spending Christmas in New Jersey. My family had not seen Heath, and it had been a long time since I enjoyed a white Christmas. We finally decided to go and bought airplane tickets.

Unfortunately, we did not tell Cheryl's parents about our holiday plans. They assumed we would be in California, and on the day before we were scheduled to fly east, Cheryl's mom and dad drove into our driveway. Mr. Friesen had been transferred to North Dakota to supervise a construction job there, and they had several weeks of vacation. I felt terrible. I had completely forgotten to keep them informed of our plans, and now I had to give them the disappointing news. They took it well, spending the holidays with Cheryl's brother Jack and his wife, and picking us up after Christmas.

In fact, because we missed Christmas with the Friesens, Mrs. Friesen felt less hesitation to stay with us after the holidays. She didn't like the cold North Dakota winter, so she spent several weeks with us. Mr. Friesen stayed only a few days before returning to work, and so missed Heath's second birthday. It was a cold night, but we went out to dinner at one of the finest seafood restaurants in Santa Cruz County, located on the municipal wharf overlooking the ocean.

When we returned, I started a big fire and we talked until nearly eleven o'clock while we warmed ourselves by the crackling flames. Then Cheryl's mother retired to the guest bedroom to read, and Cheryl and I went to bed and watched television.

A little before midnight, we heard Cheryl's mother get up and walk to the kitchen for something to drink. When she walked back down the hall, she checked on Heath, who was asleep in his room, and closed all the doors. About ten minutes later, I decided to get a glass of milk. I knew nobody was up, but I was in the nude, so I sort of crept toward the kitchen. As I passed the door to the living room, I thought I saw a flash of light in the mirror on our antique buffet. I was curious about it, but I went on to the kitchen for my milk and looked again on my way back to the bedroom. I still thought I saw a reflection in there, and I decided to look more closely. I put the glass down, got up, and walked around the corner of the L-shaped living room.

The next thing I knew, someone hit me over the head with a lamp, and I was thrown up against the wall. Then someone else grabbed me, and I threw a punch as hard as I could. When I hit him I could feel his jaw shattering. The blood splattered all over the place, and he let out a scream. He went flying over our blue chair. Then someone else grabbed me from behind and started to choke me. I reached back, grabbed his head, and ducked down, pulling him over my shoulder, and he went flying over the other side of the table and chairs. As he got up and started to run, something came down on top of my head and knocked me unconscious.

I later learned that they had hit me with an antique chandelier. Cheryl and her mother heard the shattering of the lamp and the ensuing commotion and ran into the living room, where they found me unconscious on the floor.

"Tom, Tom, can you hear me?" someone was saying as I regained consciousness. The person was down on one knee and was shaking me.

I looked up and saw a woman in a uniform, and then I looked down at my naked body. "What are you doing here?" I asked as I reached for a pillow off the sofa to partially cover my nakedness.

Whoever had broken into the dining room had stolen some of

our family silver. They had placed the silver in an antique lamp and were going to carry it out of the house in a tablecloth. Fortunately, they had to leave in a hurry and left a lot lying on the floor and trailing down the street. Cheryl was hysterical. We had been resting quietly, and someone had had the audacity to break in while we were in the house. It really frightened her. Perhaps she was most frightened by the fact that we were awake and didn't even hear the burglars. In fact, Heath could have been hurt or kidnapped, and we wouldn't have known it. His bedroom was on the other side of the house next to the living room, and the dining room was on the side of the house by our bedroom. If we couldn't hear burglars in the dining room, how could we possibly hear intruders in Heath's room?

"They were a bunch of beginners, and they never expected anyone as big as you to come walking in on them," the sheriff said. "They just got frightened and dropped everything and ran. Thank God it was you, Tom, because if it were your mother-in-law, they probably would have killed her."

Because I had a slight concussion and had strained my back in the fight, I was admitted to the hospital again.

The next weekend there was a big article in the paper about the drug problem in the area and the related crimes. Evidently, those who needed money for drugs would check out a house and break in later. Because burglars could see our sterling silver through the sheer draperies, they made our house a target. They planned to take the silver to a van and melt it down. After the pieces were melted, there would be nothing for the police to identify.

9

Come Join Our Church

Jim Cojanis, Cheryl, and I were driving through the Santa Cruz hills on a bright afternoon when I saw a highway patrolman's car on the side of the road. "I've got to see what's wrong," I told Cheryl.

"Oh, Tom, can't you just have one day off, just to relax and take it easy?" she complained.

"Let me just see what's wrong. Hang on."

At that time I worked with the Felton volunteer rescue squad, and I thought I might be needed. I got out and walked to the patrol car. As I looked down the bank, I saw a man with an injured leg. I scrambled down the bank and learned that the highway patrol was just about to move him. I looked at his leg and diagnosed that it was broken, and I told the police that if he were moved he would incur a compound fracture. I set his leg and came back to the car as he was being carried to the ambulance.

I always wanted to serve others, but for some reason I seemed to avoid the ministry. So when Pastor Carlson asked me to consider helping in his church, I said I wasn't sure the Lord wanted me to do that. I liked Pastor Carlson, and I would have loved to work with him, but sometimes the Lord has things for us to do other than what we think we would like to do.

After praying about it for some time, I told Pastor Carlson that I felt the Lord leading me toward a church that was similar to the Catholicism in which I was raised. I had been attending the Episcopal church at which Father Joe Kennedy was the rector.

Pastor Carlson was happy that I had made the choice to serve God totally, but he seemed concerned about the problems I would face in the Episcopal church. He had a special interest in me. In fact, he treated me as he did his own children. Nonetheless, I began to spend most of my time with Father Joe Kennedy at the local Episcopal church. We had become very good friends and had played golf, talked, and ministered together. After several months I began the process of becoming an Episcopal priest.

The whole church had to vote on me, and I was recommended for ordination. Then the Bishop's committee met and voted to recommend me for ordination, and Father Kennedy wrote a letter saying that I had been called to speak the gospel. He recommended me for ordination and sent letters to the committee from people who had nothing to do with the Episcopal church: Pastor Arvid Carlson; Bob Gray, the vice president of County Bank; Ron Jones, at that time president of the Felton Business Association; Dr. George Gibson, an administrator at the University of California; and Jim Cojanis.

After all those letters of recommendation, I sent a résumé of my experience to the Episcopal Diocesan at Grace Cathedral in San Francisco and to the Archbishop on Ordination. Those materials were reviewed, and a recommendation was made to review my file. I was then invited to meet with two members of the board of ordination. They recommended that I be a candidate, and I was invited to meet with the standing committee on ordination in October 1975 in Grace Cathedral, San Francisco.

The complexities of the application for ordination had become frustrating by that time. *Lord, all I want to do is serve You*, I prayed. *I feel like I'm going through the worst investigation I've ever experienced.* I was glad the day of my interview with the ordination committee had finally come.

After an opening session, I was scheduled for forty-five minute interviews every hour, except lunch, until 5 P.M. I was interviewed by a professor from the seminary at Berkeley, a minister on ordination, an ordained woman priest, the head of the ordination committee, a psychiatrist, and a bishop.

The ordained woman priest wanted to know what I thought about the ordination of women. "I have no hard feelings against that," I said, "but I just don't feel that a woman should be ordained."

That was not the response she wanted to hear. After her I met with the head of the ordination standing committee. By the end of the day I had also met with the psychiatrist. He interviewed me for an hour and a half and concluded that if any man was qualified for ordination, I was. However, he said that I showed signs of repression of hurt, and that because of this repression I was extremely tense.

The bishop and I talked for about an hour. "Tom," he said to me, "I think you're going to be an excellent minister. I think you're very well qualified. You've got a long life to serve the Lord."

Then I met again with the head of the committee. "Things look great, Tom," he said. "You've made it. Congratulations. Welcome aboard."

Everything was set for me to go to Berkeley for my final training, but I didn't hear anything for six months. I finally called the office.

"You're scheduled to come in on such-and-such a date," an office spokesman told me.

Several days later, I received a letter acknowledging that God had called me to the ministry, but saying that I could do a better job in the evangelical field. The committee did not believe I was ready for ordination. They had rejected me for the full-time priesthood, but they urged me to continue as a lay priest.

The letter took me by surprise, and I wanted to know why I hadn't been considered ready for ordination. I called several committee members and learned that many were not happy about the decision. However, after thinking about the decision and praying for guidance, I recognized that God had called me to another ministry.

Father Kennedy was shocked by the committee's decision. "Stick it out," he said. "It's people like you who are going to help change the church, change what's going on up there."

I appreciated his encouragement, but I felt the Lord had other plans for me.

Meanwhile, we had completed plans for our new house, and we broke ground in March 1976. It was a lot high on a mountain overlooking Felton. We felt fortunate to have such a beautiful site and to have such good neighbors. I had bought the lot from a good friend.

Unfortunately, our optimism gave way to incredulity as we faced one problem after another in the construction of the house. We broke ground in March, and construction went smoothly for several weeks.

Then, when the house was half built, the county placed a red tag on our building permit and wouldn't let us finish construction.

"You have an illegal water share," a county official told me.

"What do you mean?" I asked.

"The developer was allowed twenty water shares on his well, and you were number twenty-one."

We got a lawyer, and through a flurry of paperwork and legal negotiation, the developer was ordered to drill a well. Our lawyer encouraged us to sue, but I just don't believe that's right.

At the same time, we had to sell our older house. It had been on the market for a year, and it seemed we would never get it sold. As the weeks passed, Cheryl grew more tense. She couldn't see how we could possibly make two house payments at the same time. As a result of the tension, we were arguing all the time. What color for this? What color for that? We were building the house ourselves, 3500 square feet, running the business, and raising a little child. On top of all that I had almost constant, intense physical pain.

Late one night I lay in bed and assessed our lives while Cheryl read. I knew we had deep spiritual needs. "We really need to pray," I told Cheryl, and described the hopelessness of the situation. As I talked, Cheryl interrupted with other points in affirmation of my feelings.

After we talked for nearly an hour, we turned off the light and lay in the still darkness for several minutes. Then I prayed and Cheryl prayed, pleading for direction and peace in our lives.

Our lives were in disarray, and we had little discipline. We struggled from one crisis to another, and this prayer was an expression of our "foxhole Christianity." We would forget the Lord when I was feeling no pain and there were no crises. However, when we became desperate and needed His help, we knew where to go. Obviously, He was gracious to us.

Finally our new house was almost finished in June 1976, and we became reconciled to the fact that we would have to be making two house payments. We took our house off the market and prepared for the worst. A few days later, Cheryl was doing some housework when she heard a knock at the front door. She opened the door, and a woman greeted her.

"Do you want to sell your house?" the woman said.

"What do you mean, do I want to sell my house?" Cheryl asked. "I'd love to sell my house." There was no sign on the lawn, but this woman real estate agent thought she would inquire about buying the house.

"We have a lady here with $10,000 cash who would like to buy a house," she said.

A few days later, another couple expressed an interest in buying the house. They just drove by, saw our house, and stopped and asked to buy it. Cheryl and I were astonished. We said, *Lord what do we do?* Finally we sold it to the woman who had made the first inquiry. She put enough money down to pay for the acreage on which the new house had been built.

One afternoon we were sitting at the table in the new house, having a cup of coffee and talking about the sale.

"Isn't that just like God?" Cheryl said. "We went a whole year and were desperate to sell that house. Then out of the blue, someone comes and buys it." There were no complications, and the woman bought it directly from us. She paid a commission to a friend.

The move went just like clockwork. It was amazing. The woman moved into our old house the same day we moved into our new house in El Solyo Heights, and our neighbors helped us move. All the people in the development had become good friends of ours during the construction of our house, and I was impressed by their selflessness.

My good impressions were modified about a week after we moved when I walked over to the house of my friend who had sold me the lot and found his wife in tears.

"I don't know what I'm going to do," she said, explaining that her husband had gotten involved in a church that was draining all their finances.

I didn't know what she was talking about, and I didn't think it was right for me to inquire when she was so distraught. I knew she had always been a devoted believer, so I was concerned about her bitterness against the church.

As I was leaving, I saw her husband near the community well, and I asked him what church he had joined. He said it was a different kind of church. I asked what kind. He'd finally found "God's bridal church," he said. He added that he'd been fed up for a long time with all the "hypocritical churches" in the area, and that he'd found a church that was honest and sincere.

After a few minutes we said good-bye to each other, and I walked slowly down the gravel road to our house.

I later discovered that many of our neighbors belonged to this church, which is considered a cult by orthodox Christians. *That's why they were all so helpful,* I thought. This church is extremely evangelistic. Our neighbors wanted to convert us to their church, so they helped us move and did many kinds of things for us during our first days in the new house.

Our neighbor's comments also explained his wife's grief. The church he had joined expects a high percentage of each member's income. Those gifts enable the church to grow, and all my neighbors were deeply involved.

From that moment, Cheryl and I prayed continually that the Lord would provide a way for us to serve them and win them to Christ.

Meanwhile, I wanted to close the business and go into the ministry, but Cheryl expressed extremely strong disapproval. She felt the business gave us a dependable income. In spite of the tremendous pressure and problems and the trouble with employees, she felt it offered us some security. I gave in and set aside my plans for the ministry.

In the early hours of the morning a few months later, I was in such pain that I couldn't get off the floor. I had thought that the firmness of the floor would ease my pain, but nothing seemed to help. I called a friend to take me to the hospital.

Cheryl was becoming tired of my complaints; she couldn't believe, even after all that had happened before, that my pain could be so bad. "Here you go again," she said. "Back into the hospital. You're never home." It was difficult for her to see me in pain all the time. She rarely had physical problems, but everything seemed to go wrong with me.

Meanwhile, my friend had arrived. He saw how badly I hurt, and he realized that Cheryl no longer understood the extent of my pain. They talked intensely, and the strain in their voices didn't help me a bit. Finally, he helped me up and took me to the emergency room of the hospital.

The doctor on duty glanced quickly at my medical file and my legs. He saw the needle tracks from injections of Demerol and morphine that my doctor had prescribed for me to administer myself at home, and they led him to the wrong conclusion about my situation. He was an internist who had been having addicts come off the streets and ask for medication. Then I came along at the end of the day, and he did not look carefully through my records. Suddenly, he felt he couldn't take another addict again, and he became very angry with me and called me everything under the sun.

"I'm not an addict," I protested. "I've got a back problem."

"I see guys like you every night," he said. "Look at you. You've got punctures all over. Get out of my room." He pulled me off the table and shoved me out the door.

I was in severe pain, and the doctor's actions humiliated me. I felt I wasn't even human.

"Let me see the administrator," my friend said. "I want the administrator right this minute."

When the administrator arrived I told him, "I'm not an addict. I've been instructed to take this medication. Your doctor humiliated me in front of at least ten or fifteen people who were in the waiting room. Call Dr. Raymond Nelson. He knows my case. He operated on me."

The administrator called Dr. Nelson on the telephone. "Did you look at his medical record?" Dr. Nelson asked. After a short conversation, I was admitted to the hospital and treated there for a week or so.

I was in the hospital many times during the next few months, and my back condition grew worse. They would put me in traction for a week or ten days at a time and give me pain killers and muscle relaxers.

My condition seemed hopeless, and I knew I had to do something. I was in the hospital one day in traction, experiencing excruciating pain, and I wanted to talk to somebody. But I didn't want to talk to the priest of the Episcopal church I used to attend.

Show me what to do, Lord, I prayed. *Help me.*

I began looking through the telephone book, turned to the church section of the Yellow Pages, and looked at all the denominations. My fingers ran over one little area subtitled

Mennonite Church, and I saw Neighborhood Church. I had never heard of a Mennonite, but I thought I'd call. I was searching desperately.

I had also made up my mind that day in the hospital that I was going into the ministry full-time. I was going to work at it. I was going to close down my business, sell out. That was it.

I closed the phone book, picked up the telephone, and dialed 475-5959. The phone rang and a voice said, "Hello. Pastor Ron."

"Pastor, I'm Tom Scarinci. You don't know me. I'm in Community Hospital. While I was lying here, praying, I felt led to call your church." I told him that I was an Episcopalian with a Catholic background, and that I was studying to get into the ministry. He was intrigued, and we talked for ten or fifteen minutes. The next day he came to visit me.

We hit it off right from the start. Ron Penner was so open that I felt I had known him all my life. We talked for a couple of hours about our backgrounds, and he was amazed. In fact, several months later he told me he found my story so bizarre that it was difficult to believe. But my vision excited him. "Tom, why don't you come and be with our church?" he asked. "People who are sick and in convalescent homes will find comfort from you because you've gone through so much pain."

10
The Only Alternative

thought about Ron's invitation after I was released from the hospital, and on a bright, clear Sunday morning in July 1976 I got up and drove to the Cliffwood Heights Neighborhood Church. I parked in the lot and slowly walked to the front door of the small church. There to greet me was a tall, gray-haired man, Jack Flemming, the moderator of the church. In the warmth of his voice I felt the presence of Almighty God. I knew that He was alive in this church. It wasn't a handshake like "Hi, how are you?" It was "Welcome, we love you."

I hadn't known it, but Pastor Ron had told the congregation about our visit at prayer meeting the previous Wednesday. He had told them I had promised to visit, so the people were ready for me, and many of them made me feel I was part of the group, and that I belonged. It was so different from the kind of churches I had previously attended, and I felt strength and support among those warm, loving people. For the first time in years, I felt hope.

I continued to attend, and after several Sundays, Pastor Ron asked me if I would teach a young people's Sunday school class. I wasn't a member of the church, but I thought it would be a way to serve. I did not get close to the young people, however. I was too intense for most of them, too preachy and mission-oriented, and they held me at a distance. Gradually I realized that I was an example of the very thing I was talking against. I was speaking for more faith and commitment by our young people, and in the process I was showing that I did not have enough faith to allow God to work in His own time and at His own pace.

In addition, back pain was an ever present element of my life. I couldn't stand up straight, and I couldn't walk unless I was bent over as though I had a terrible stomachache. Repeatedly I would have to call Pastor Ron and cancel my Sunday school class. I knew I was not being dependable, and I wondered how Ron could put up with me.

The months went by, and I was in the hospital at least two more times. But instead of resenting my illness or calling me irresponsible, the people at the church encouraged me and treated me as an equal. I was amazed at the way they came to visit me. Their love and support had a tremendous impact on me, and I drew closer and closer to them, wanting more and more to be a part of that body.

By January 1977, my pain was so intense that I often could not think of anything except enduring through the next minute. The thought of the next hour or the next afternoon was more than I could bear. I was in agony all the time, and only pain killers kept me going. I lived on them.

My condition was so bad that I hardly did anything with the business. Cheryl ran it, and I devoted more and more time to the Cliffwood Heights Church. As a result, Ron asked me to attend a minister's conference at Mount Herman. The messages I heard there were inspiring, and on the drive home Ron and I talked about programs we could implement. Times such as these were crucial in getting me to look beyond my condition.

One night I didn't get home until about 11:30 P.M., and it felt really good to just sit down and discuss with Cheryl some of the thoughts I had received at the conference. We talked for about fifteen minutes, and then I heard a strange noise outside. I thought it may have been our dog, but I wasn't sure.

"Something sounds funny out there, Cheryl," I said. "Did you hear Shane whine or howl?"

"No."

"I'm going to check." I picked up the shotgun and looked out the back door. "Did you let Shane off the porch?"

"Yes."

"Well, I can't find him, and he's not answering."

I shut the back door, walked to the front door, and shined the flashlight around the yard. Then I heard more whining. I shined the light about forty feet in front of me, and I saw Shane hanging by a rope tied to a tree branch. *Oh, Lord, they've killed Shane,* I thought.

"Call the police," I yelled to Cheryl. "Someone just hung Shane."

I ran to Shane and lifted him up. The rope from the tree branch was tied to a wire and wrapped around his neck. The wire was so high that I couldn't get enough leverage to lift him free and work it loose. In desperation, I grabbed the whole branch of the tree, pulled it down, and broke it. Quickly I untwisted the wire, eased it over Shane's neck, and carried him into the house.

By this time the police had arrived. They beamed their flashlights all over the yard, looking for footprints or some evidence, but they didn't find anything.

"There are occult groups in the area," one of the sheriff's deputies said. "They cut open and sacrifice animals."

Our property bordered on Fall Creek State Park. A lot of transient people were sleeping in the parks. In fact, Santa Cruz County was having problems with whole groups of communes gathering in the parks. We concluded that some occult group had randomly selected Shane to be hung or had wanted to get even with me for teaching a Sunday school class about the cults and occult groups, warning our people about the dangers of their practices. The former seemed more probable, but we were so jumpy that we really couldn't think straight.

Cheryl was especially upset. "It's bad enough to be the victim of a robbery, but to hang a dog is just hideous," she said angrily. We had an eerie feeling that there was something demonic in the area. We didn't know what kind of element we were dealing with.

Later, about four in the morning, we heard another noise. "What was that?" Cheryl asked.

"It sounded like a car," I said. "Where's our car?"

"It's in the backyard," she said as she rushed to look out the window. "It's not there," she called.

I shoved on my slippers, scrambled into my robe, and ran to look outside as Cheryl called the police again.

The patrolmen followed tire tracks through the backyard to the edge of a forty-foot embankment, where they saw our car.

We had locked the doors, but someone had used a device to open the door on the driver's side. They had put the car in neutral and pushed it down the hill. "You thought we were gone," the culprits seemed to be saying, "but we're still here, and we're watching you."

That incident really scared Cheryl. I don't think I had ever seen her so terrified. Whoever had hung the dog had also pushed the car into the ravine, and we knew they could be hiding in the wooded area around our home, watching us. We felt our mountain was infested by the occult and we no longer could be secure, so that perhaps we should place our dream house on the market.

In fact, Cheryl had become nearly hysterical. She felt she couldn't take any more. I had been sick for months. The business had been the object of petty thefts many times. Our house had been robbed; our car vandalized; our dog hung. It was just too much to bear.

During the evening, I had reinjured my back lifting Shane down, and I began to feel the pain after I calmed down. I called Dr. Scibetta on the phone, and he told me to be admitted to

Dominican. Cheryl drove me there, but she was afraid to stay alone in the house while I was in the hospital. She called her parents, and they arrived in the afternoon. The next day Cheryl's brother and family drove from Santa Rosa to celebrate Cheryl's mother's birthday and Heath's birthday.

Fortunately, Cheryl's mother stayed with her for several days so she didn't have to stay alone in the house. They visited me each night at the hospital and then drove home. Cheryl and her mother would circle the property with the car and flash spotlights all around. Then they'd park the car and let Shane go in the house first.

You can imagine how alienated Cheryl must have felt. My physical condition seemed to be deteriorating, and people were terrorizing her to the extent that she was afraid to stay in her own house. It was as though she had no home. When Cheryl's mother left for Florida, where Mr. Friesen was supervising construction, a friend came to stay with Cheryl.

After a week's stay, I was released from the hospital. By this time I had been in the hospital more than twenty times since 1972. I was beginning to face the fact that I was never going to get over my back trouble. The doctors couldn't seem to remedy my condition. All they could do was put me on drugs to cope with it. Each time I had even a small jar, I grew worse, and often I went through extremely traumatic situations.

However, about this time Mrs. Andrews, one of our customers who had a lot of problems with her back, told me about Dr. Robert Hass in Palo Alto. He was a wonderful doctor, she said, with more than twenty years of experience. I mentioned Dr. Hass's name to Dr. Scibetta. He thought about it for several days and then recommended I go to the pain center in Palo Alto. He sent all my records there, and the pain clinic mailed me a lot of forms. They wanted me to go to a psychologist and take about two hundred dollars worth of psychiatric tests.

"That is ridiculous," Cheryl said. "I've worked with these tests, and they are not going to solve your problem. You know what's going to happen to you? It's going to be just like all those other times you went to the doctor. They're going to take this stack of medical records a mile high, give you all those psychiatric tests, and they're not even going to look at you again. You ought to go to Dr. Hass cold turkey. Don't take any records with you. Nothing. Just go up there."

Mrs. Andrews made an appointment for me to see Dr. Hass in March, and I was admitted to the Hoover Pavilion at Stanford University Medical Center. They did tests on me every day for about two weeks. The staff was really nice to me, but I just couldn't stand being in a hospital. If the staff had not been so considerate, I don't think I would have made it. I had a private room, and the staff let Cheryl bring Heath up every night. They would give him a soft drink, and he would watch television while Cheryl and I talked.

Cheryl would drive an hour and a half through the traffic to visit me for half an hour. Then she would drive home, go to bed late, get up early in the morning to make lunch for Heath and herself, drive to work, take care of the shop all day, and then drive to see me in the evening. Her schedule was inhumane, but what made it so bad was that I kept getting worse. There seemed to be no end to my problem. They tried all different kinds of things, and they talked about a delicate surgical procedure that might ease my pain, but which could also cripple me.

"No. Absolutely not. I can't take that chance," I said.

The doctors released me from the hospital, and Dr. Hass prescribed a vigorous schedule of exercises. He ordered me to swim about four miles a day, lose weight, and just baby myself. He reminded me that I would be disabled the rest of my life, and that I should accept that fact and act accordingly. He didn't want me to be tearing limbs down to save a dog that had been hung, or to fight with burglars. I had to live like an invalid.

Within a few days after this hospital stay, we decided to

go see Cheryl's grandmother in Washington. She was extremely old, and we wanted Heath to see her before she died. Meanwhile, after much thought and prayer, Cheryl and I reached a big decision. It seemed that every time I was supposed to teach my Sunday school class at church, I was in pain. I never knew if I would feel good enough to meet my responsibilities, and I felt I was letting Ron down. I decided to write a letter of resignation to the church.

The trip to Washington really extended my patience. I couldn't drive, and I couldn't sit for very long. It was just awful.

Fortunately, Ron did not accept my resignation, and I continued to work with him and the church when we got home. But the constant medication was affecting my ability to think, and when swimming, losing weight, and other therapy did not work, I once again seriously considered suicide.

Dr. Laubscher had given me a prescription for seven shots of Demerol one afternoon when the pain had become particularly unbearable. I couldn't wait to get home and take those shots. I put the small paper bag down on the kitchen counter and took out a small plastic container with enough for one shot. I carried it into the bathroom and gave myself an injection. I waited a few minutes, but there was no relief. I took another shot and then another. I took a lot of medicine in three hours, but I still hurt. Gradually I realized that I had taken several doses. It must have been three doses. Things were going. It was as if I couldn't see. I was falling all over everything.

I got up, and I was crying. I felt my way into the bathroom, locked the door, and took a vial of 30 cc of Demerol. That's enough to kill a person, especially if it's injected into the bloodstream.

I took a syringe and filled it for the lethal injection. As I held the needle to push the fluid into my bloodstream, I saw a bubble in the syringe. For some reason I paused and pulled the needle out of my arm. Then it hit me. I was trying to commit suicide, and yet I was afraid of a bubble in the syringe. What difference did that make? If I intended to kill myself, why was I so afraid to die?

Whatever the reason, seeing that bubble brought me to my senses, and I stopped my suicide attempt. I took the needle, threw it into the toilet, and flushed it away. I lowered the toilet lid and sat down. *You're crazy, Tom,* I thought to myself. *You've got to get to a hospital.*

As I began to think about what I had done, I seemed to become more and more aware of the irrational and desperate nature of my condition, and I couldn't control my emotions. I cried like a baby.

I wanted to talk about what had happened. I went into the bedroom and started talking to Cheryl, but she was asleep and didn't even hear me.

I sat on the bed for several minutes, thinking, *What do you want from me, Lord?*

I couldn't go anywhere. It was the middle of the night. I was in a corner, and I knew what the Lord wanted.

All right, You've got it, I prayed. *I can't depend on anything anymore. I don't know where else to go. Do You want me on my knees? Do You want me on rock bottom? You've got me there.* I hoped the Lord was satisfied now.

Do something, I told Him, *but don't make me go on this way anymore.*

After several minutes I got sick to my stomach, and I went into the bathroom. I felt terrible.

I've had enough, I said to myself.

I went back to the bedroom, pulled my .38 caliber pistol out of the bureau drawer, and loaded it. I walked back to the bathroom to end it all. As I looked out the bathroom window, a bright light flashed through the sky.

I know it sounds phoney. As I think back on it now, I

wonder whether I wasn't just going through a process of proving to myself that I didn't have the pessimism to kill myself. But at that time, that shooting star was a reality, a sign that God was with me.

I had not really wanted to kill myself, but I hurt so bad that I no longer could think straight. I seemed to be able to accept any excuse to avoid death, and I took my finger off the trigger and returned the gun to the bureau drawer.

The next morning I went to the church to talk to Ron and hand him another letter of resignation.

"I know that the Lord gives 100 percent of Himself," I said, "but I can't give 100 percent in return. I never know when I'm going to be able to go to church. I'm just not dependable."

"Tom, I don't want your resignation," Ron said. "As far as I'm concerned, you're giving 100 percent of yourself."

Then I told him what had happened the night before and that I had made a radical decision. I had decided to go through a surgical procedure that could remove the pain but that might paralyze me.

"Are you sure you want that, Tom?"

"Yeah."

"You realize there's a 50 percent chance you may come out paralyzed?"

"I know, but I'm going to do it. I'm a vegetable now, and I can't go on this way. Last night I wanted to die, and I'll be that way again when I'm alone and in pain."

Ron Penner would be perfect in a typical Hollywood movie as the good, kind, young minister with good looks who, with a pretty young wife, takes a struggling congregation and helps it become a growing, unified body of believers. He is a trim, brown-haired man who dresses neatly and speaks well. He hated for me to have pain, but he wasn't sure that I was making the right decision. He was afraid that I might be causing myself greater pain than I had now. He wanted to make sure that pain had not twisted my thinking processes.

"Whatever happens, I want you to know that the Lord loves you," Ron said. "If He has called you to His service, He'll enable you to serve."

"I've thought of that a hundred times," I replied, "and I'm going to call my doctor today."

There was a 25 percent chance I would come out with the problem corrected, the ability to walk, and the pain gone—but no feelings in my legs. The other 25 percent chance was that I would come out the same as I went in.

Arrangements were made, and surgery was scheduled for May 17, 1977, at the Stanford University Medical Center. Dr. Hass was to be the surgeon.

Cheryl opposed the surgery. "I'd rather have you the way you are than paralyzed all the time," she said angrily.

"I've got to go through with it," I explained. "I am as good as an invalid the way I am now."

After a few days Cheryl realized the strength of my resolve, and she called her mother and asked her to stay with her and Heath while I was in the hospital. However, Cheryl's parents had just moved to Florida, where Mr. Friesen was supervising construction of a refinery, and Cheryl's mother just didn't see how she could afford to fly to California, as they had not yet recovered their moving expenses. She had intended to come to California during the summer, though, and she promised to spend several weeks with us.

Cheryl accepted her mother's decision, but she told me she didn't know how she was going to live alone in the house. That night, however, her mother reconsidered her decision, and in the morning she called to tell us she would come. She says now that it was the Holy Spirit who told her to come, whether the trip could be afforded or not. She arrived on May 15, 1977, the Sunday before I was supposed to have surgery. I was to give a devotional in church that day, but my pain was too great, and I stayed home.

The next day I felt better, and I helped Cheryl landscape our property. Here I was a day away from delicate back surgery, and I was bending over, stooping, shoveling, lifting—just doing all sorts of painful things that aggravate injury to a back. I would get so excited about such a project that I would be like a football player during a game, and I wouldn't feel the pain until later. We thought shrubbery would help us sell the house. It had been on the market four months, and we had not had any potential buyers.

Also, I knew that Cheryl had wanted shrubbery for a long time, and I felt guilty because I had not done anything sooner. I wanted to prove myself to her. It might be the last thing I ever did; that thought really gave me enthusiasm for the project. But I have to admit that at the end of the day, when I drove my pickup truck from the lumberyard with wood chips, fatigue was taking over, and I was beginning to feel the throbbing pain. I spread the chips around the bushes, hung up the rake in the garage, slipped out of my work shoes by the back door, and lay down on the carpet in the family room. I ached all over, but I felt a sense of accomplishment. I knew Cheryl would be happpy.

11

Judgment and Forgiveness

Ron called Monday morning before I went to the hospital.
"Tom, how are you doing?"

He was afraid I could be having second thoughts, and he
wanted to be of help if I needed it. I think he was surprised when
I quickly replied, "Fine."

We talked for several minutes about the church and his dream
for my ministry. Then he suggested we pray.

I don't remember his words, but I did feel confirmation that
this surgery was God's will, that He was in charge. It was a
moving prayer, and when Ron said amen, there was a brief
silence. Then I said, "Just remember, Ron, no matter what
happens, no matter how I come out—I'm going to serve the
Lord. I'll be in God's hands. Whatever His will is, will be—
even if I don't come out of it at all."

"I feel no fear in your voice, Tom," Ron said huskily. There
seemed to be something in his throat, and this expression of
friendship and warmth gave me a sense of strength in the Lord.

Later, as I was getting ready, I told Cheryl I wanted to drive
in by myself. I hadn't been driving for almost a year and a half,
and Cheryl was surprised by my comment.

"How can you drive an hour and a half? You never drive,"
Cheryl said.

"I just want to be all by myself," I explained. I kissed her
good-bye, picked up my suitcase, and got into my blue pickup

truck. I backed out of the parking space by our house and waved as I pulled slowly onto the road.

After I left, Cheryl drove to work. She thought she could keep her mind off me if she kept busy. Fortunately, Nancy Jorgenson walked into the shop that afternoon. Nancy and her husband had visited the shop several weeks earlier. As we became better acquainted, a friendship was developing. Jerry was a pilot for Airwest and they were extremely gracious people. Heath had gone to their house to play a few times, but we didn't know each other well. Nancy may have come to the shop more to visit than to make a purchase—I really don't remember—but during the conversation, Cheryl mentioned my surgery the next day.

"Why don't you let Heath stay with me?" Nancy asked. "The kids will love it."

That night Nancy called and said, "We'd love to have Heath stay overnight with us." Cheryl appreciated the offer, so she packed a pair of pajamas and some clean clothes for Health to play in, and Nancy picked him up Monday night.

About two hours later, Cheryl called me at the hospital, but there was no record of my being admitted. She waited for another hour and called again, but I still hadn't arrived. Cheryl was becoming extremely worried. She called every hour three or four more times, but there still was no record of me.

Finally she learned that the linkage had broken on the truck, and that I had had to walk a mile to a service station to get the car towed and the linkage fixed. I didn't arrive at the hospital until nearly dark, and I spent the night by myself.

Dr. Hass came in during the evening. He couldn't believe the faith and excitement I had about what was going to take place. I knew the Lord was going to take care of my problem, but Cheryl did not share my confidence.

Cheryl was anxious and short-tempered Tuesday when she went to the shop to tie up some loose ends. When she had done that, she taped a note to the door, saying that she would be back on Wednesday. She locked the shop and picked up her mother, and they drove to Palo Alto. When they walked into my room, they were surprised and a little angry to find me joking and having a great time with the nurses. They were extremely nervous, and I was acting as if nothing unusual was about to happen.

"How can you joke at a time like this, Tom?" Cheryl said. "You're going in for major surgery that could change your whole life, and here you are, clowning around like a kid."

"Honey, I'm scared, but God will take care of me. I can't worry about what will happen. I won't know until it's over. But no matter what happens, life will be better. I can't go on the rest of my life this way. And if I have one chance to do a better job for God, I'll do it."

"I understand," she said, and nodded.

"I'm not going to give up. I've got a chance, and I'm going to serve the Lord."

"I understand," she said, but I saw the furrowed brow and the anxiety. Cheryl felt so badly for me, and she understood the gravity of the situation all too well.

"If it means that I've got to take a chance on my life here or be paralyzed or whatever God wants, I'm going to do it," I said.

Dr. Hass walked in as we talked. A friend of his son was in the emergency room after a motorcycle accident, and Dr. Hass had to set a pin in the boy's leg. As a result, my surgery was going to be delayed.

"Cheryl," I said, "you and your mother go out and have lunch, and don't worry about me. When you get back it will be all over. I know everything will be all right."

After some insisting on my part, she said she would go. "Is there anything you want?" she asked as she picked up her purse.

"Yeah. Bring me a big Genoa salami."

"What?" she asked in astonishment.

"I'm going to be hungry. You know they're not going to be

giving me anything. I'll be on IVs. Bring me a big salami."

"Tom, it's sure to be four or five dollars a pound," she protested.

"You just do what I tell you," I answered, and she and her mother left reluctantly. After she left, it dawned on me how worried she must be. Cheryl is thrifty, and she had to be very upset to agree to spend four dollars for a pound of salami, much less the price of a whole salami.

About an hour later, a nurse entered my room and gave me a shot.

"Give me some more of that stuff," I told her. "I want to know I'm out. I don't want to know anything about it. I want to be out."

"Don't worry," she said as she left the room.

A few minutes later, another nurse opened the door. "We're going to take you to the surgical suite," she said as a green-clad attendant rolled a cart up beside my bed. He pulled down the side of the cart and helped me from the bed. In a moment I heard the click as he slid the side back into place, and soon we were gliding silently down the hall.

Everybody was joking and smiling at me when I was wheeled into the prep room of the surgical suite. They were in gowns and had masks on their faces, and they started to shave my back. The anesthesiologist walked up to the cart and said, "I'm Dr. Walker." He had visited with me the night before to let me know what he would do. "I'm going to put some stuff in your arm, and I want you to count down," he said.

"Doc," I said, looking up at him, "make sure I'm out."

"Don't worry. You'll be out."

"That's what they all say," I answered. "But I'm weird. I don't go out that easy. So give me a large dosage before I go in that room and somebody cuts me open."

"Don't worry. Now count out loud for me."

"One, two, three, four, five. . . ." I had reached ten, and I still wasn't out.

Dr. Walker realized I needed an extra dose. "Good-bye," he said. That was all. Whatever he did, he did it all at once, and I went out.

At that point I didn't know what was going on. Then, in what seemed like a few seconds, I felt a change in my body. I couldn't breathe, and I heard a turmoil around me that frightened me.

I had gone through operations before, and I knew something was wrong, but I had never sensed such intense turmoil before. I was gasping for air, and the feeling terrified me. I prayed for help.

I was in another state. I no longer was a sleeping body. I could see and hear what was happening. I saw the blur of white and blue gowns running around and I saw anxious faces, but I don't remember what took place from the time I went out until the time this traumatic thing happened.

As I look back on it, I left the normal realm of consciousness for something that no one understands. I could see myself from inside my body, but I could also see things that were happening throughout the area.

During the ten days that I was unconscious, I remember people becoming Christians and people being united in prayer. The most beautiful part was that people were being united. I saw people in the hospital praying for me—people from all over praying for me. I saw my church getting together to pray for me, and I realized that no matter how useless I was, no matter how hopeless, what was happening to me wasn't important. But because of my experience, people were becoming united and very close to God. I began to see the beauty and joy that came about because of what was happening to me. Because of my illness my family was drawing closer together, people were growing in faith, and people were learning about God and trusting in Him. Then I realized how it must have been for our Lord to see His Son suffer, to see Him nailed to a cross.

In the operating room there was panicked commotion. Dr.

Walker's face was worried, and I knew I was dying. There were tubes and all sorts of paraphernalia around the table as they worked on me.

"What's going on here?" Dr. Walker asked, checking me and the equipment.

"What's happening?" he yelled.

Then he whirled around. "We're losing him."

I felt pounding, and then I felt a jolt. Dr. Walker put things on my chest. Then he kept saying, "Come on. Come on." I remember his yelling.

I felt more pounding on my chest. Then I remember someone else taking over and doing the same thing. One person pounded for a while, and then another took his place.

"We're not going to get him. We're not going to get him. We're going to lose him."

"We've lost him."

"No. We haven't lost him yet."

I could hear the exchange among the doctors, and I was really frightened. It seemed as if the room were spinning and lights were flashing. There were all kinds of bright lights and confusion around me. Total confusion. People running around. People complaining. Then I remember a doctor's calling for somebody. Then someone left the room. I don't know who it was, but the man who left the room was the one who said, "We're not getting him back. We've lost him." It might have been Dr. Hass. I couldn't say for sure.

"What are you doing?" someone yelled. "Move it! Get over here! Move it! Come on! Get over here!"

Something tore at my chest again, smashing me in two. I was crushed. Then I started to fade out, and I became even more frightened. I faded away deeply, and a warmth came over me. I felt something hot touch my shoulder. It was a deep touch that I could feel throughout my body. It was like every inch of me had been completely taken over. Then I felt something raise me by my shoulders. I keep using the term "touched" because it felt as though someone walked up and literally comforted me by putting his hands on my shoulder. I felt totally at peace as I have never felt in my entire life. Every problem in the world looked trivial. I had no worries. It was as though I were translated from one state of being to another. I didn't even think about the surgery any more. I focused on the beauty around me, the people, the families. Everything was changed.

Then I heard "I'm with you, my friend," and I saw a bright light. It wasn't like lights that are outside. It was like a sky full of lightning. It was a glittering brightness that hurt my eyes. I can't even describe it. I don't have the words. How can you express something so beautiful? How can you compare it when there's nothing on earth like it? But it was just as if it surrounded me, and I was being drawn into it. I was in the hospital room, but I saw it all there, and I felt the presence of Almighty God. There seemed to be direct communication between Him and me, and the brightness was engulfing me.

Soon I was floating. I didn't feel as though I had left my body, but as if I were floating.

I prayed fervently. I prayed and prayed. I didn't see anything in the hospital room now, but I knew everything that was going on. It was almost as if God had stepped into the room and surrounded everybody. There was a light breeze about me.

Gradually this all passed for a moment, and I felt I was standing with the Lord, talking to Him and asking a lot of questions. But He wasn't saying anything back. I just knew everything He was saying. I didn't have to ask. He was revealing everything to me.

"Why? Why now?"

Suddenly I realized, "Man, you've had it. You're here."

I knew it wasn't a dream. I must have died, I thought. That's when I started thinking of all the good things I had ever done for the Lord.

That ended quickly, and soon I saw myself as a little boy

maybe two or three years old, and my whole life rushed past me. It wasn't an orderly vision, with something happening on one day and something else on another day. Instead, everything was visible at once. Every little thing I had ever done wrong was spread out before me—a terrifying instant replay of sin and selfishness.

It was obvious what the verdict was going to be. I was guilty, and I begged the Lord to forgive me.

Suddenly I knew that God is totally forgiving. I was kneeling on something like a cushy pillow, and I was lifted up and felt His forgiveness.

"Thank you, Lord. Thank you. Thank you," I said.

I knew for the first time that He was so forgiving. Yet I was so ashamed that I had thought I had done good deeds for Him. I wanted to take everything I had given to the Lord and hide it. It was so small compared to what He had given. Then I felt I had cheated Him. I saw what He had invested in me compared to what I had done for Him, and I knew I had cheated Him. I didn't know how to repay Him, but I wanted a second chance.

I asked Him not to take me yet, not because of my wife, not because of my family, but because I wanted to serve Him again. I wanted to let people know that their real life is in Christ.

Then the light got even brighter. It was blinding in its intensity, and I prayed earnestly to God to forgive me, to help me to serve Him better, and to show me that this is where He wanted me. Then someone said to me, "Son, in losing as in winning, there will be much more suffering in your life."

I said I didn't care, and the light grew even more intense. The brightness was indescribable, and I could feel a wind—almost as if it were blowing through me. It was a feeling of freedom.

While the wind was blowing, I could see a bright figure in front of me. I fell to my knees and bowed my head. Slowly I looked up and saw a human form wearing a red robe with gold trim and a gold crown. I couldn't make out any features, but the figure looked like a person I had seen many times. I don't know who I saw. I was frightened, and I kept saying, "Forgive me, forgive me."

Then the figure took my hand and said, "I'll always be with you."

When I was in that state of no measurable brain activity, I was able to look objectively at everything happening around me. For example, Jim Cojanis came into my room and heard all the bad news. He heard my mother and everybody else crying. He insisted that despite the way things looked, I was going to be all right.

One of the doctors became angry with Jim because he "wouldn't deal with reality." I heard a group of doctors talking about him on the other side of the doorway, in a coffee lounge. They would often sit there and discuss my case.

The doctors laughed and teasingly argued with Jim as he tried to witness to them. After a while the doctors began to get annoyed and they mocked him, but he didn't realize it.

I wanted so badly to be able to say, "Jim, you can't shove it down their throats. Be realistic."

I felt sad only once during the ten days. That was the afternoon my son Heath visited Cheryl at the hospital. Early in the evening, Cheryl told him he would have to return to Felton with the Jorgensons. He couldn't understand that. He wanted Cheryl and me to go home with him. I could see Cheryl's pain as she knelt in front of Heath in the lobby, and I could see the incredulity of my two-year-old son. My grief was almost unbearable. It was the deepest grief I've ever felt.

On another occasion I saw nurses arguing over who was going to take care of me. I was hanging onto life by a thread, and the nurses were bickering over who was going to have to change the bed, change my drain, and so on.

"Oh, that's your job," one said.

"You do it," said another.

"I'm not going to do it."

They didn't care about the patient. All they cared about was getting away without doing the dirty work.

I was having bowel movements at the time, and they had to put a bedpan underneath me. They didn't like that.

"Let what's-his-name do it," one of the women said. "I can't lift him all by myself. I'll just wait until someone comes."

"No one's taking care of him, and no one has changed his stuff for a while," a black-haired nurse said. "Someone's got to get over there."

"Oh, I'll get to him. He's not going anywhere."

At least one nurse saw no point in helping me. "Why don't they just take him out of here?" she said. "He's gone. Why don't they let people die in peace instead of playing games?"

"Well, they still have hope," the black-haired girl responded.

"That's what I don't like about religion," another nurse replied. "It goes too far. Why don't they just face the fact that he's gone?"

The black-haired nurse often took care of me, and as she worked she talked angrily. "Where's this God of yours?" she would say. "Why doesn't He help you?"

There was a girl on the left side of me. She walked away and the black-haired girl lingered. "God help this man," she said. "He's too young." She prayed for the Lord to help me, and tears rushed down her cheeks.

"God, why him?" she went on. "Why do you have to take this young man away from his wife and family? If You're up there, God, show me. Make me see that You can do something to help this man."

"This is a lot of nonsense," another nurse said. "Why don't they take him out of here now? He's going to be a vegetable." She kept saying that a bunch of hypocrites were coming in and praying and saying that God was going to do some kind of miracle.

One of the doctors got tired of my being kept on the machine.

"He's not going to make it," he said. "Let's stop this charade."

Jim Cojanis had come in with brother Dave Fast, a deacon in the Cliffwood Heights Neighborhood Church, and my mother. Jim, who believes very strongly in faith healing, suggested that they all pray for God to restore me.

Evidently Dave Fast was not so sure they were praying in the Lord's will, and the next thing I knew, Jim was insisting to Dave that I was going to be OK. I knew Dave was not convinced.

"We're brothers in Christ," Dave said, "and we both believe in the same thing. The important thing is not our differences right now, but that we unite together in prayer for Tom."

During the entire ten days, it was almost as though God gave me an opportunity to look at the world from His point of view, and it was frustrating because the petty bickering dominated the discussions around me, and I began to dream that I was tired of the racket. "I'm going to make it," I dreamed. "No way am I going to lie around on this bed," and I dreamed that I sat up.

Everybody in the room looked at me.

"Don't get excited," a nurse said. "This is typical of how a person gets when the end is near. He gets exuberant."

"What do I have to do to prove it?" I said to myself. I started stretching my muscles: one, two, three, four, and kept doing it to regain my strength. I was going to prove to them that I could do it.

"Take it easy, Tom," someone said. So I lay down, and soon I had pneumonia, and the nurses were laughing and saying, "He thought it was going to be a miracle. You notice he didn't make it."

After I regained consciousness, I asked Cheryl about the incident. She said it never happened, but it had seemed real to me.

12
Where Is Your God?

During the ten days in which I had no brain waves, Cheryl went through the most difficult period of her life, being confronted by the fact that her husband was as good as dead. After the hectic activity of those first few hours started to wear off, she began to realize the importance of events, but she was having difficulty collecting her thoughts. She slipped quietly into the hospital chapel. There she complained and begged and thanked the Lord. And, after a long time, she began to realize a sense of serenity and strength that enabled her to resist the doctors who wanted to take me off the life support equipment.

In the previous chapter I described my perceptions during those ten days as I lay on the "cooling bed" and yet could observe incidents happening in many parts of the hospital—indeed, throughout the area. Now I want to relate what happened to Cheryl. She described these events to me after I had regained consciousness and told her my story.

She and her mother had begun the ten days by shopping for some curtains and eating lunch at a neat little restaurant near the hospital. When they returned at 3 P.M., I was in surgery, so they walked to the waiting room near the surgical suite. There they were somewhat surprised to find Ron and Fran Penner. Cheryl had told Ron not to bother to make the drive to Palo Alto. She had been through hospital visits so many times that she didn't think this trip would be any different. But Ron and Fran came anyway and brought their children to be with Cheryl and her mother.

All of them were together in the waiting area near the surgical suite, drinking soft drinks and laughing, and the Penner children were playing with twin girls.

"Stat. Stat. Stat," the loudspeaker called, and then several doctors' names were called.

"Something must be going on," Cheryl said.

There were heart transplant and open heart surgeries each day at Stanford, and she thought one of those operations was having complications. They never related the activity to me because my surgery was not expected to endanger my life.

Then there were more calls on the loudspeaker.

Fifteen or twenty minutes later, a little after 4 P.M., Dr. Hass came out of the surgical suite and walked over to Cheryl. "Are these people with you?" he asked.

"Yes," Cheryl said.

"Would you come over here with me," he said, and took Cheryl by the shoulders so that the others couldn't hear.

"I want to tell you, we lost Tom," he said. "He had a cardiac arrest. I don't know what happened to him, but we lost him on the table."

Then he told my mother-in-law to call my family and get them to California right away.

"What about the surgery?" Cheryl asked.

"We're not doing the surgery. We're working on him right now."

Cheryl knew the surgery was not life-endangering and so started laughing, but Dr. Hass firmly grabbed her arm. "Listen," he said. "Tom's had a cardiac arrest, and his heart isn't working. We're working on him right now."

Cheryl looked at Dr. Hass intently, searching his face. *What's he telling me?* her face seemed to say. *Dr. Hass is serious, but how can it be?*

Then Dr. Hass began to talk again, and Cheryl realized her

husband's life was in jeopardy. She held Dr. Hass's hand tightly as he explained that my heart had stopped and they had not been able to restore a regular heartbeat. Generally doctors do not continue heart massage for an extended period, but I was young and muscular, and the doctors wanted to exhaust every possibility before giving up on me.

Dr. Hass talked for several minutes. Then he returned to the surgical suite to see if a regular heartbeat had been restored. "We're going to put a gauze in the back of him and just sew him back up. Then we'll let you know," he said. The indications were that when he returned he would have to tell Cheryl I was dead.

Months later he would not confirm or deny that he said those things, but there were two witnesses.

"I just can't believe what he said to you," Fran told Cheryl. They just sat there, and one of the pink ladies stayed with Cheryl as they waited.

It isn't possible, Cheryl thought. *Dr. Hass must be mistaken. He must be talking about some other patient.* But it wasn't a mistake. It was real, and they were stunned as they sat in confused silence while the doctors battled for my life.

Cheryl called Nancy Jorgenson to see how Heath was doing and to tell her that the surgery was taking longer than expected; it didn't look as though they'd be home for dinner.

"Don't worry about it," Nancy replied.

A little bit after 5 P.M., one of the doctors came out and told them they were moving me to respiratory intensive care, a room within the intensive care area for heart patients.

Cheryl, Ron, Fran, and Cheryl's mother went to the waiting room outside, and there were doctors everywhere. After a few minutes, Dr. Myer Rosenthal walked up to Cheryl. "He's had a cardiac arrest," he said. "His brain has been without oxygen for a long time. We're going to keep him here." He wanted to comfort Cheryl, to help her feel secure. He was trying to spare her from the bizarre reality that I was as good as dead and that there was no hope for me to live a normal life even if I survived. He told her they wanted to try an experiment, a new technique that had not been used on many human beings. It was a procedure used on people who had experienced oxygen deprivation for an extended time. He indicated that the procedure was the best chance for me to live.

"Just ask me questions whenever you feel like it. I want you to know what's going on," he said. He didn't ask Cheryl for her approval to do the experiment. He just told her, but she approved. She wanted the doctors to do everything they could.

Immediately they gave me an injection of thiopental sodium and placed me on a "cooling bed" that would lower my body temperature. All this had taken place within an hour after a regular heartbeat had been restored.

The doctors told Cheryl I probably wouldn't wake up, but that if I did, it would be within twenty-four hours, and I would be severely brain-damaged. Later they extended it to forty-eight hours, but they couldn't tell at that point how badly brain-damaged I would be. They made it clear that there would be no use in Cheryl's planning on my being normal.

Cheryl was confident I would regain consciousness. She felt it would be all right. She just didn't know how I would take being brain-damaged, especially if I were severely retarded. She thought I could cope with being in an iron lung. I had had to cope with so many things before, and we really hadn't had a bad life.

As she walked down the hall from the waiting area, she slowly entered the last doorway on the right. To the left were a coffee pot and chairs where relatives could sit, and to the right, a telephone, a medicine chest, and four beds in a row. I was in the last bed, and three post-operative patients were in the first three.

Cheryl was stunned by the setting: each of us was hooked up to all sorts of monitoring devices, and we all had tubes down our throats. My situation was somewhat different from that of the others. I lay on a "cooling" bed, with only a cloth covering my genitals.

A doctor patrolled the area, monitoring each patient's condition. In front of my bed was a nursing station. It looked like the cockpit of a giant airplane, with all sorts of video display terminals and a myriad of switches. The paraphernalia covered the room and gave it a crowded feeling.

The whole scene was more than Cheryl could handle. She had been to medical school, but she had never seen some of the equipment they were using on me, and she was not prepared to see me unconscious, kept alive by the miracles of modern medicine.

In a few minutes Dr. Murray Walker, the anesthesiologist, entered the room. Tears streamed down his face as he tried to explain what had happened. He brought my chart, but his grief overwhelmed him, and he sobbed bitterly.

"It's not your fault," Cheryl said. "It's all right."

"No, it is my fault," he said. "It is my fault."

Through the years I had taken so many pain killers that it took a heavy dose of anesthetic to put me under. Dr. Walker wanted to make sure I was unconscious. As a result, he felt he caused my cardiac arrest by giving me an overdose."

"No, it's really okay," Cheryl said, but he continued to sob.

"We named our son after you," she told him. "Heath Walker Scarinci." She made that up to try to make him feel good. She was trying to talk to him about anything and everything. He had been a doctor for more than twenty years, and nothing like this had ever happened to him before. His sense of failure was intense. Even three years later, his voice would break when he talked about the incident.

Dr. Walker is a sweet, loving man, so different from some of the other doctors who didn't seem to care about what happened. In fact, two years later, one of the doctors asked me if Cheryl had ever forgiven him. He knew she had not appreciated his behavior. He'd pat her on the head when he saw her and say, "It's going to be OK."

But Dr. Walker felt anguish. In fact, he felt so bad that he did not take a vacation. Instead he came to the hospital every day, and Cheryl and he would talk. It was fortunate that Dr. Walker was so upset, because Cheryl could keep her mind off herself. Instinctively, she tried to comfort him. She felt she was keeping him "up" every day. She tried extremely hard to have a happy face when he came around. She knew he was taking it too hard, and she could identify with his sense of loss.

While Cheryl was sitting in the room with me, her mother made calls to my family in New Jersey. She called Aunt Elnor, my mother's sister, but Aunt Elnor wasn't there, and my grandmother answered the phone. It was midnight eastern time, and my mother-in-law did not want to upset my grandmother. She talked a few moments and then hung up without leaving a message.

"Call Cookie's husband," Cheryl told her mother. Cheryl hadn't even told them I was going to the hospital, so it would be a surprise for both Cookie and Jerry. But Cheryl knew Cookie would be extremely upset. She knew Jerry would listen calmly and respond appropriately.

Unfortunately, Cookie and Jerry had an unlisted telephone number. Cheryl's mother didn't know this, and she called information and got the number for their son, Jerry, Jr. She called, and a male voice answered. She thought it was Jerry, Sr., and she was so upset that she didn't realize she was speaking to the son. Eventually Jerry figured out that she wanted to speak to Jerry, Sr. When she finally talked to him, she was confused. They talked for several minutes before he understood that I had suffered a cardiac arrest and that the doctors thought I had no chance for survival. She explained that the doctors were going to put me on a bed packed with ice and thus lower my body temperature.

Jerry and Cookie were shocked. They didn't even know that I was in the hospital, and now they got the message in the middle of the night that I was as good as dead. The unpredictable brother was in trouble again. Cookie and Jerry made calls to the family, and my brothers and sisters began calling the hospital. They called every few minutes for hours. Finally, the nurses at the station refused to take any more calls, and Cheryl felt she couldn't talk to anyone on the phone. The irrepressible anxiety of my family had so irritated the nurses that they were in a nasty mood.

Cheryl and her mother stayed at the hospital almost all night. They sat in the lobby and walked back and forth down the hall. They didn't dare leave. They were afraid the doctors would take me off the life support equipment, yet they found it terrifying to see me. There were so many tubes and machines, and I lay there cold and nearly naked like a corpse in a morgue. They couldn't stay in the room very long without weeping.

Nonetheless, Cheryl spent hours in the room, sitting by my bed, holding my cold, lifeless hand.

By the time they had been at the hospital fifteen hours, Cheryl's mother realized she needed to get away. She sensed it would be several days before my condition would be clear.

"Let's get a motel," she suggested to Cheryl.

"No, let me sleep here."

They talked about it several times as the night wore on, and Cheryl's mother finally got her way and started calling motels, looking for a room. She must have gone through three dollars worth of dimes. Finally, one of the nurses in intensive care found a motel room for them in Redwood City, and they left the hospital. It was about three or three-thirty in the morning by the time they signed in and got to their room, but Cheryl couldn't sleep. She felt sick to her stomach.

The abrupt reality of the inevitability of death was so close that life itself had been unreal. She wanted to relax. She took a hot bath and tried to accept the fact that she might never have her husband back alive and active. Only a few days before he had been planting bushes and spreading wood chips. Now he was little more than a cold hunk of flesh on a cold table.

After her bath, she dressed and walked down the hall to the vending machine to buy two soft drinks. She filled a bucket with ice, returned to the room, lay down on the bed, and she and her mother sipped the soft drinks and talked. Cheryl didn't try to plan her life, but she did think about a funeral for me. I had always wanted to be buried in New Jersey, and she decided to have my body shipped back.

They were tired, but their nerves were jangled, and they could not relax. They knew that my life was very precarious. They could not sleep. At about six, just three hours after checking in, they drove back to the hospital and began another long day of waiting.

During the morning, the nurses and staff people cleaned up the patients and changed bed linens. Cheryl and her mother waited with relatives of other patients in the waiting room. Many of them had traveled thousands of miles to Stanford, and friends and relatives of patients often stay for weeks. They became acquainted and encouraged one another.

A couple named Arnold told Cheryl's mother that there might be room in the Riviera Motor Lodge, a motel close to the medical center. Mrs. Friesen called and was fortunate to get a reservation for the last vacant room. Mrs. Arnold's brother also was in respiratory intensive care, and the Arnolds became close friends with Cheryl and her mother as they shared experiences.

Mrs. Harrington was also an inspiration. She had undergone a heart bypass operation and was an amputee. When she saw Cheryl and Mrs. Friesen waiting for news, she forgot her own problems and stayed with them.

A young couple who lost their thirteen-month-old baby after a bypass operation spent hours praying for me as their son's condition worsened.

Mrs. Meyers had a son in the hospital. He was about twenty years old and was extremely sick. He had some kind of terrible heart disease, and he wasn't going to live. She and her husband were distributors for a candy company. Every day they would pass around big candy bars. The Meyers were a constant source of strength and support. In fact, when people talked to Cheryl, they thought Mrs. Meyers was a relative.

There were many others who provided support to Cheryl and her mother. Many of them were Christians. Cheryl was overwhelmed by all the Christians and other loving, caring people who strengthened her during those torturous days.

Every morning when Cheryl arrived at the hospital, she would see how I was, and her mother would visit with the relatives of the other patients and ask all the people how their patients were.

On that first morning, Cheryl contemplated the fact that I might never be sound again even if I lived, and she wanted to get away from the noise and activity of the ward to be alone to collect her thoughts. She asked three people where the hospital chapel was, but they didn't know. Finally she got directions and made her way down a maze of corridors, hallways, escalators, and stairs, through carpeted rooms lit by fluorescent bulbs, to the huge, bustling main lobby in the front of the medical center. There to the right of the reception desk is a hall to the outpatient clinic, the emergency room is straight ahead, and a stairway to the other floors is to the left.

Cheryl walked through the busy lobby toward a little door. She paused to make sure it was the right door. Then she turned the knob and left the noise and endless activity, entering a tiny, dark room not much bigger than a walk-in closet. It was furnished with a few short, wooden pews, the walls were a dark walnutlike paneling, and the carpet was a deep crimson. At the front was an altar and an open King James Bible. The Twenty-third Psalm was printed in big letters on the front wall.

Cheryl felt extremely alone as she walked slowly to the front, knelt at the altar, and began to pray. She started slowly, but once she got going, she let God know everything she felt.

Tom has really been a terrific person, she prayed. *He's been a great husband and a wonderful father. I really have no complaints. Maybe it would have been nice if he hadn't been sick all the time, but it's OK, Father. It hasn't been that bad.*

She wanted the Lord to know how grateful she was for the good things she had. But she also wanted the Lord to know that she wanted Him to do His will for her life.

If there ever were a person who wanted to go to heaven to be with You, he does, she prayed. *You take him.* Then she was quiet and thought about the seriousness of her prayer. *But, Lord, we have a beautiful two-year-old son. Please take care of us alone.*

Thank You, Lord. Thank You for putting Tom in the hospital. Thank You for all our problems. She wanted to say it, but she didn't really mean it.

God, You know I don't mean this, but You're going to help me mean it, she said. *You're going to help me be faithful in all things that happen. I trust You that You're going to make me believe what I'm saying.*

As she meditated, time passed, and she sensed a special quietness.

Gradually an acceptance came over her. *It's OK with me,* she prayed. *I've been married for five years and have this little child, and Tom really wants to be with You, Lord, because he believes in Jesus, Your Son. So it's OK with me if You want to take him.* But she also prayed that I wouldn't be retarded if I did wake up.

You know, God, whatever You want is OK with me, she said. *I really don't have a right to pray for something for me. Whatever happens, You just do Your thing, whatever it is.*

Then she was quiet for a long time. She had made her peace, and after many minutes she got up, a strong person again. A tremendous peace surrounded her. She had made the decision that she wasn't going to be sorry any more. She wasn't going to stew and fuss. She had given up her problem to God—completely. *God, it's all right,* she prayed. She had given her husband to the Lord, and she knew she could go on. She never took back her problem.

People always try to preach, "Give it to God. Don't worry about it." But that's easier said than done. Cheryl had tried it every day for years. She'd say, "OK, God, here it is. You take the ball and run with it." But then thirty seconds later she would be thinking about the problem again. However, she really did give her burden to God that morning in that tiny chapel in one of the greatest medical centers in the world. It was a moment that changed Cheryl's life. She would never be the same. She had finally made an absolute commitment to the Lord.

When she returned to my unit, she received a call from Cookie, telling her that my brother Albert and my mother were flying out from New Jersey and would arrive that evening.

"That's all I need," Cheryl said, seeming to lose her sense of peace. "I'm holding myself together by a thread. I just can't hold other people together, too." She had a very bad attitude about my mother's and brother's coming. She felt she already had more than enough to try to cope with, without having to worry about the problems others were having in dealing with my condition.

Albert and my mother arrived in San Francisco at about nine that night and called Cheryl at the hospital.

"I'm renting a car," Albert said. It was pouring rain, and he wanted to know which way to come.

"How far are we from the airport?" Cheryl asked one of the nurses.

"About twenty to twenty-five minutes," she said.

"Do you think I should leave?" Cheryl asked. "What if he dies while I'm gone."

But they couldn't answer that, and they never said yes or no. Cheryl and her mother decided it would be all right, and Cheryl told Albert and my mother to wait in front of the terminal.

They waited about thirty minutes before Cheryl picked them up. Cheryl hardly knew them, and they felt strange learning of my condition from a virtual stranger. They were quiet as Cheryl drove through the rain toward the hospital.

Cheryl tried to prepare them for what they would see. She told them they might be upset when they saw me. She explained that the doctors said that if I were going to wake up it would be within twenty-four hours, but that even then I would have severe brain damage or be a vegetable. However, those first twenty-four hours had passed, and now they were saying it would be another twenty-four hours.

Despite Cheryl's words of warning and preparation, Albert and my mother were overwhelmed when they walked into the room and saw me. My mother turned white.

''Where is your God now, Tommy?'' she asked. ''I've never seen so many tubes and machines. I watch 'Marcus Welby' and 'General Hospital,' but I've never seen anything like this.''

That's when Cheryl became third in line at my bedside. Albert and my mother pushed ahead of her. Albert teases her now and says, ''Oh, were you there? We didn't know that.''

Meanwhile, everyone else in the family called every half hour or so. The phone seemed to ring all the time. In desperation, the nurses told Cheryl and Albert that they couldn't have any more phone calls. One nurse became extremely angry at Cheryl. It upset Cheryl because she wasn't asking anybody to call; my relatives just were very worried.

13

Why Can't Daddy Come Home?

Day after day it was the same. The machine was breathing for me, and the doctors didn't have anything to report. There had been no change one way or the other, and it was practically hopeless. On Friday, May 20, Dr. Hass made his rounds, patted Cheryl on the head, and said that my condition was getting better. A few minutes later, Albert and Cheryl were standing by my bed when Cheryl spoke to a woman doctor.

"Dr. Hass told me he's getting better," she said, seeming to want confirmation. "He's getting better, isn't he?"

"No," she said as she looked at Cheryl. "He's getting worse. He's not going to make it longer than an hour or so. Even with all the life support equipment, he's not going to make it."

Cheryl considered that an unnecessarily abrupt rejection. She felt the doctor's hostility toward her hope for life, and she began to cry. She had been told one thing by our doctor, the man who was supposed to be taking care of me. Then she entered my room, and another doctor told her the end had come. She was hurt and confused. She wanted to hang on to the ray of hope that she had been given by Dr. Hass, and she sobbed hysterically. She couldn't calm herself. Then Dr. Rosenthal walked by with a group of residents and interns. He saw her sobbing and came back a few minutes later to talk to her. He put his hands gently on her shoulders, pulled her forward, and pressed his forehead against hers.

"I'm sorry," he said, "but you're supposed to be a professional. We can't keep him on this equipment any longer. I tried my best. It was an experiment, and it didn't work. He's not going to make it. He's got pneumonia, and his blood gases are extremely low."

He could tell that Cheryl was dazed, that his words were not sinking in.

"Listen, Cheryl, he has no brain waves. He would be a total vegetable even if he woke up, and you can find a new husband and father for your son. You don't want a vegetable.

"There's no possibility of his being normal," he explained. "His brain was without oxygen for an hour.

"Straighten up. You've got to be stronger than this. He won't live through the night. He's just too far gone because of the pneumonia. If it were up to one of the doctors, he would have been covered up a long time ago.

"You might just as well decide you have to get a new husband and father for that little boy, because he's not going to make it."

Cheryl's mother overheard him and became extremely angry. She called Jim, and he said he'd come up right away.

Before he arrived, Dave and Agnes Fast came walking down the hall into the waiting area. It was during the worst time, about four in the afternoon. Cheryl was still sobbing hysterically after her confrontation with Dr. Rosenthal.

The Fasts were extremely encouraging when we first came to Cliffwood Heights Neighborhood Church. They always had newcomers over for dinner; that was their ministry. The people in our church take seriously what the Scripture has to say about visiting the sick and shut-ins, and now, in Cheryl's greatest hour of need, the Holy Spirit had directed this older couple to be with her.

As they entered the room, the nurse asked if they were family.

"Well, sort of," Dave said. "Brother Tom and I happen to be members of the ministry in the same church, and I'm a deacon, so we do feel like family."

"In that case, you are very much needed."

All the tubes and life support equipment seemed to take them aback as they stood over my body. All Dave could see was a dead man, and he quietly began to cry. Agnes couldn't stand looking at the body any more, so she left the room to comfort Cheryl.

Dave's head was bent as he sobbed softly. Then he reached out and touched my hand. It was the hand of a dead man, cold and lifeless, and he knew I was dead. In that moment he asked the Lord why.

For many minutes he stood, sobbing. Then he was still, and he seemed to accept my condition and turn his thoughts inward. *Are we being selfish, praying for the survival of this man?* he asked the Lord. *Maybe it's not Your will, God. Maybe You want to take him and we're being too selfish.*

A nurse came over to my bed and asked Dave to step aside. He had forgotten there were other people around, so the nurse's whisper startled him. Then he looked at his watch and realized that he had stood by the bed for more than an hour.

He moved haltingly toward the end of the bed. "What does it look like?" he asked the nurse.

"It's hopeless," she said, and he began to weep again. He saw a nurse take a pin and jab me to test for reflexes. My body did not move. Then she held a mirror against my mouth, and there was no sign of breath. Finally she spread my eyelids and shined a beam of light in my eyes to see if my pupils dilated when the light was turned off. There was no dilation in either eye. Clearly, there was no room for hope.

Dave's shoulders were stooped and he walked as though he were very tired. His face was almost expressionless, stunned by the realization that his brother Tom was dead.

Meanwhile, Jim Cojanis had arrived at the hospital and met Cheryl's mother in the front lobby. He tried to assure her that I would pull through.

While Dave stood at my bed, Agnes came to Cheryl. Agnes had been a widow. She knew that because Cheryl was young, she would certainly remarry and find a father for Heath. She wanted Cheryl to know that she wouldn't be the first person to be a widow at twenty-seven years of age with a small child.

She told Cheryl her son had been sick, and she had given him up to the Lord. Both Dave and Agnes had lost marriage partners by death before their present marriage, and she was trying to tell Cheryl that she could find someone else eventually.

But Cheryl didn't want to think about that possibility. The thought of marrying someone else disgusted her. "Well, I'm really not the right age," she said. "That's great for older people who want companionship. I'm a young woman with a child."

Dave and Agnes both talked to Cheryl about how they had lost their spouses through death, and about how hard it was. They understood how Cheryl was feeling. Dave made small talk for a long time with Cheryl's mother and mother-in-law. Finally, after Cheryl had calmed down, Dave suggested that they all pray. He wanted to ask God to answer prayer, but he felt so selfish. He thought he was praying against God's will. If ever there was a dead man, Tom was that man, and God seemed to be showing that He wanted Tom.

Jim didn't feel that way, however. He thought they could demand my life, and he was persistent in saying so. Gradually, there was a meeting of minds.

"OK, we're all in agreement then," Dave said. They all stood in the hallway, held hands, and prayed. Dave started the prayer, and they all prayed in turn. It wasn't a long time, maybe ten minutes, but it was an unusual event for that hospital to see people praying. They weren't used to that.

The essence of their prayers was that they would give me up to be with the Lord if He pleased. But Cheryl was adamant about trying to keep me alive. She would not let the doctors take me off the machines, so they could not take me to the morgue at that time. By evening the crisis had passed.

Later in the afternoon, my mother turned to Cheryl and talked about Jim's prayer. As they talked, Cheryl described Jim as a Christian.

"What's a Christian?" my mother asked.

Cheryl answered, telling her what it means to be a follower of Jesus Christ.

Then a neighbor couple came to the hospital. They were very, very good friends of ours, very strong in the cult religion to which many of our neighbors belonged. They explained that their church believes that when a man who has been anointed by God dies, he will be resurrected as a god. The man asked Cheryl if she would allow me to be anointed with a special cloth.

"I know we don't believe alike," he told Cheryl, "but I love Tom."

Cheryl's blood turned cold. She and I had been praying for this neighborhood couple. She turned to Jim. "What should I do, Jim?" she asked.

"I don't know," he said.

Cheryl was almost panicky, but it didn't show. She stared at the wall and prayed. *Dear God, if I ever needed You, I need You now. You know how Tom liked these friends. What do I do?*

Then these words came to mind: "It's OK. I'm in charge."

It was as clear as if she were talking to someone. She said yes, and our neighbor went to the head of his church—not just the local church, but the entire church—and received permission to use the anointed cloth. He brought it to the hospital.

"Tom, God will be with you," he said. "I hope you understand that what I'm doing is letting the power of the Holy Spirit work within you." Then he laid the cloth over my face.

Cheryl felt sick to her stomach the whole time. Later, Jim said he thought she made the right decision. "God is bigger than any cult," he said.

A lot of our friends went into the room and began praying,

and Christians throughout the area were praying. One nurse called her mother, who was a Christian. The nurse told Cheryl that a lot of churches in the area were praying for me. There had been many calls to the hospital from churches in the area. The word had gotten out that a Christian minister had gone through a cardiac arrest and was lingering on life support systems but showing no brain waves. As the story was told, thousands of Christians came to my support. They didn't know me, but they knew my God. He was their God, too, and they believed He could heal, that He holds the life of each of us from moment to moment.

At about ten that night, Cheryl and all the others were in the lobby, and the doctors told them they had injected pure alcohol into my lungs. They said I had shown a little bit of improvement in my battle against pneumonia. My temperature had been 108 degrees, but the crisis had passed and they now thought there was a little hope concerning recovery from pneumonia. But my general condition was still extremely critical.

Excitedly, our neighbor gave credit to the power of the anointed cloth. He was convinced that I would come back to life and become a resurrected god.

That night, Cheryl and her mother read portions of Scripture from my Bible and prayed for the Lord's direction. As they leafed through the Bible, they found my notes for the talk I was to have given in church the previous Sunday. The subject was the morning prayer of David from Psalm 3:1-8.

My case was particularly interesting to the nurse in intensive care because I was so young. They all were about Cheryl's age. Many had young children, and they thought that any of their husbands could be lying their instead of me. One girl was pregnant, and she was trying to think of a name for her child. Cheryl suggested she use Heath.

Every day people would come up to Cheryl and tell her they were praying for me. The pink lady who had been on duty when

I was undergoing the cardiac arrest visited with Cheryl for several minutes each day.

As Cheryl walked down the hall, people would say, ''There's that girl.'' Then they would tell the whole story. Everywhere Cheryl went, people knew who she was.

One of the nurses who worked that Friday night came to Cheryl later and said she believed in God because I was still alive.

The wife of a man in his early thirties told Cheryl that my situation had made her realize how thankful she should be. Everybody in the intensive care unit was extremely sick, but countless people came to Cheryl and told her how thankful they were that at least their relatives weren't as bad off as I was. That may seem cruel, but it was a source of comfort. Cheryl realized that the way she reacted to my situation was a source of strength for others, and that knowledge helped her to rely on the Lord at all times.

The nurses fed me big injections through the nostrils. They'd give me delicious malts. I loved them, but one time they gave me a strawberry malt, and I had stomach pains because of the strawberries. I know it is difficult to understand how I could have pain when I had no brain waves, but I did. Every time I was pricked with a pin, I felt it. I just couldn't react to let the doctors know that I felt it.

Saturday, May 21, Cheryl's brother Jack arrived from Santa Rosa. She had not been close to him in recent years, and she really appreciated his coming. When Jack saw that nothing much was happening, he said to Cheryl, ''Nothing's changing, and Albert and his mother have not seen your home in Felton. Let me take them there.''

Cheryl's mother went with them. She picked up our mail, the checkbock, and a few clothes for Cheryl, who had only the clothes she was wearing. She had intended to return to Felton the night of the surgery and had not brought a change of clothes. Her teal blue pants, beige shirt with a teal blue diamond pattern, and teal blue vest had become a familiar outfit.

When Jack and the others returned to the hospital, I was a little better. My temperature was lower, and there were several other hopeful signs, so the doctor told them to go out for dinner. Jack took them to an exclusive Chinese restaurant in the San Francisco area.

There were seven of them at a table for eight, and the empty chair was between Cheryl and my mother. That deeply affected my mother. She sobbed softly throughout the meal because of that reminder that I was not with them.

As much as Cheryl didn't want anyone to visit the hospital, she was grateful for them, especially Albert. She and Albert became very close. They sat in the cafeteria for hours, and he would tell her about things he and I did when we were young. He helped her to feel she was accepted by the family. He told her how grateful the family was that she married me. I had been unhappy in my earlier marriage, but the family knew how happy I was married to Cheryl. Cheryl really enjoyed Albert's versions of the stories, because they depicted Albert as the hero. In all my stories, Albert was the troublemaker, and I was the hero. Those were wonderful conversations, but even they could not overcome the tedium of the hospital stay.

Day after day, hour after hour, the time dragged. Cheryl and Albert would look at their watches and think that at least two hours had passed, when in fact it was no more than five minutes. They were waiting at one of the world's famous hospitals. Outstanding doctors said that I might wake up in twenty-four to forty-eight hours, but I didn't wake up. The wait seemed like an eternity, one day stacked on another.

While they sat at the end of the respiratory intensive care unit, they would hear a dietary presentation given to those who were going home after heart surgery. After two presentations a day, Cheryl could repeat the dietician's presentation verbatum within a day or two. She knew the whole speech by heart and had fun making the presentation. But she also got angry when the patients complained because they couldn't eat salt or have a martini. A few years earlier they would have been dead, because open heart surgery didn't even exist then. Cheryl would have given anything for me to be recovering from open heart surgery instead of lying naked without brain waves.

"You people should be so thankful," Cheryl wanted to scream. "Even if you can't eat anything for the rest of your life, who cares? You're alive. You've got a chance on life."

She vowed that if we came through this crisis, we would never forget it. She told the Lord that if I lived through this we would see to it that we had more time for family recreation, that we would put more time aside for each other. Heath was just two years old then. He loved to go to the park and feed the ducks. He begged us every day during the week before I went into the hospital to take him to the park, but we never had any time. Cheryl knew she was fantasizing because she knew I would be a vegetable even if I did wake up.

Throughout the entire ten days, Cheryl never really felt defeated, but on the Monday after the surgery, May 23, she became extremely distraught. She ran out of the hospital and walked back to the motel. Albert saw her leave and followed her. He knew she was upset and depressed and wanted to be by herself, but he thought he might be needed, so he decided to follow her at a distance. She walked through the large shopping center near the hospital and then walked back to the motel. It was a long walk, but it enabled her to be alone with her thoughts and work off her nervous tension. It helped her to feel better.

The waiting was intense because there were no daily chores to do. The family could only wait and wait. While they waited they prayed, ate, or shopped, but it seemed they did more eating than anything else.

The doctors had urged both Albert and Cheryl to talk to me, and to relieve the tension of waiting, they both said many things to me. Cheryl told me I could shave my beard and that she would learn to play cards. She detested playing cards, but now she would do anything for me. She even promised not to nag me anymore.

Her promises were well-intentioned, and they gave her hope, but my condition worsened. The doctors cautiously tried to tell her that there was no hope, that it was ridiculous to continue this charade, this phoney belief that I would regain consciousness. She had been tenacious. It had been her aggressive refusal to allow the doctors to disconnect me that had kept me on the life support systems. She would not even consider it, but a week had passed, one day after another, and there still was no sign of life. Cheryl was down psychologically and totally exhausted.

Tuesday, May 24, sitting by the coffee pot, she wavered and consented to let Albert have my Bible. Albert stood up and picked the Bible off my bedside table, and two pieces of paper fluttered to the floor. They were the notes that my mother-in-law had found a few days earlier.

Albert looked at the passage. He couldn't believe what he read:

"O Lord, how my adversaries have increased! Many are rising up against me. . . . I lay down and slept; I awoke, for the LORD sustains me" (NASB).

It was a quotation of Psalm 3:1 and 5, a psalm of David.

"My brother knew this was going to happen to him," Albert shouted. "He knew this was going to happen, and he knew God would take care of him."

Everybody gathered around and read the portion of Scripture. Then they read my notes and turned to all the Bible references that were mentioned. Suddenly there was hope, a message of faith in a time of despair, a message of life and resurrection. But most of all, Cheryl took it personally as a clear sign from God that He would bring me back. Now there was no thought of taking me off the machines. They agreed that it was too soon to carry me off. The doctors got very upset, however, because they thought the "nonsense" was going too far.

All my friends said, "Let's pray."

"Let them go ahead and pray," a nurse said. "They need it more than ever now."

"This is ridiculous," one of the doctors said. He said some vulgar words and turned to Cheryl. "He's going to be a vegetable if he wakes up, and that's it. Let us take him."

Moments earlier, Cheryl might have consented. She had been sitting by my bed, sobbing, seeing me for the last time before they wheeled me to the morgue. But now she was firm in her resolve that the Lord would let me live.

"No, sir," she declared. Nothing would shake her.

The two pieces of paper had turned a moment of farewell into a time of prayer and hope. Perhaps no one was affected more than Albert. He knew that I believed God was going to take care of me, and he wanted everybody to know. He tried to reproduce the two sheets of paper, but none of the available machines were operable.

The impact of those pieces of paper was so strong that nobody would dare take me off the life support equipment. To do so would have been against the mood of those who visited the hospital every day. It would have been a failure to believe. It would have been just plain inhuman. Even those who did not believe in God would not have been so brazen.

Another crisis had passed without Cheryl's giving her permission for me to be taken to the morgue. There was new hope, but my family was exhausted. The tension just could not continue much longer at such a pitch. How long could Cheryl keep the doctors from relegating me to the morgue? Would a crisis soon come that would end this vigil? Those were some of Cheryl's thoughts as the night passed and she slept poorly. Her burden was heavy despite renewed hope.

The next morning, Wednesday, May 25, Cheryl spent some time at my bedside with Albert. When medical students started their routine checks, she decided to take a short walk. She just had to get away by herself every so often.

Walking heavily down the hallway, she seemed oblivious to

the scream of a nurse. Then Albert burst out of the room.

"He moved! He moved!" Albert shouted ecstatically.

A medical student had taken my temperature, and my leg had twitched. Albert and Dave and Agnes Fast had seen me twitch.

You would have thought that I had been raised up like Lazarus. There still was no indication that I would live if I were taken off the machines, but it was the first time any muscle movement had occurred. It was enough to make my friends more enthusiastic, but Cheryl was realistic. She knew it didn't mean much. She was looking for a real sign. She expected me to regain consciousness, and she did not know how long we would have to wait. She was confident, but she didn't know how long she could hold the doctors off. Nonetheless, the day passed quickly. There were at last tangible signs of improvement, and they occurred throughout the day as I continued to move.

Still the doctors did not offer much hope. "It doesn't mean anything," they said. "He's 500 percent better than he was, but he's still in critical, critical condition."

Later, Albert, now even more influenced by the pieces of paper that had fluttered out of my Bible, drove to Menlo Park and paid for photocopies. When he got back to the hospital he ran from room to room, telling the story of how I had moved and handing out copies of my notes.

"My brother knew," he kept saying. "My brother knew that God would take care of him."

That afternoon Cheryl, Cheryl's mother, Albert, and my mother took a quick trip to San Francisco and Fisherman's Wharf. Usually it's impossible to find a parking place, but after a short search, they were able to park. Cheryl's mother is very conscientious. She believes a person should obey the law and that society should serve law-abiding citizens. They filled the parking meter with enough money to last for days. But when they returned about twenty minutes later, they had a parking ticket. In San Francisco at that time a parking ticket was twenty dollars, and Cheryl was not about to pay a fine for something she did not do. She ran up and down the street, looking for a phone. She called the San Francisco Police Department and told them what happened. Then a squad car drove by. They stopped the policeman and showed him that the meter was broken. It showed expired on one side and four hours worth of parking on the other side.

"I can't do anything about it," the policeman said, "but I'll remember it."

Cheryl's mother insisted that Cheryl write down his license number, and after a lot of correspondence, the ticket was waived several months later.

That evening the Jorgensons brought Heath to the hospital. Cheryl met Heath in the lobby, and she cried until her nose turned red and they hugged and hugged. Heath seemed so small and so innocent for the stark reality of death. Here was a familiar face, our young son, the antithesis of death, our hope for the future. Here was the personal expression of Cheryl's and my love. Cheryl felt that moment deeply.

After she had talked with Heath for several minutes, he went with his grandmother and uncle to visit in their motel room, and Cheryl talked with the Jorgensons. She was so grateful to these friends who had cared for her son. She hardly knew how to tell them.

"We've enjoyed having him," Jerry told Cheryl. "He's so well-behaved."

They described their good times with Heath, and Cheryl felt the depth of their loving care for our son.

"Our only worry has been that he's so young, and he might not get the relationships right," Jerry said.

Heath had been calling Jerry and Nancy "Mommy" and "Daddy." Nancy told me how badly this upset Jerry. He was afraid that Heath was forgetting Cheryl and me. He told Heath to call them "Mommy Nancy" and "Daddy Jerry."

The hospital visit helped Heath and Cheryl get reacquainted and helped Jerry feel confident that Heath had not forgotten

Cheryl and me. He was merely showing respect.

After about an hour, Jerry and Albert went out for a pizza. When they brought it back everyone had supper, and then the Jorgensons prepared to leave. But Heath did not want to go without Cheryl and me.

Cheryl tried to explain that I had to stay at the hospital and she had to stay there with me.

"Why can't Daddy come home?" he asked. "He's been in here a long time."

"Daddy's still very sick," she tried to explain, but she didn't think he understood. "He's very sick, and he may have to go be with Jesus," she continued.

"Why? I want my daddy to come home."

"Don't you understand?" she said. "God loves Daddy, and Daddy had to go to live with God. I don't think God is going to let Daddy come home again."

Heath just couldn't get it into his head. He said, "God loves me. So why won't He let my daddy come home?"

"Heath, your daddy has gone to heaven. He's going to be in heaven."

Cheryl was torn between two positions. She didn't know what to tell Heath. She didn't want to tell him I was coming home, but she didn't want to tell him that I wasn't coming home. She just wanted him to realize how serious my condition was, and it hurt her so badly to see the simple faith of her son and feel his grief.

The hospital worried Heath, and he tried to be so grown up. After that day, he often asked Nancy if they were going to visit Heath's mommy that day. He wanted to visit Cheryl, but he didn't like the hospital. In fact, he's still frightened by hospitals.

The doctors suggested that Cheryl place photographs by my bed. They thought pictures would help me remember if I regained consciousness, and also give me a sense of security.

Cheryl took their advice and had some photos brought from home.

Wednesday night I continued to move and twitch, but brain waves still had not been restored. How long would I remain unconscious? Only four persons had ever lived more than twenty-four hours, and only one had regained consciousness and not been severely brain-damaged.

Thursday morning, May 26, the vigil began again. About mid-morning, Albert sat in his usual place near my bed and watched a nurse pour a malt into one of my tubes. As she poured, I opened my eyes.

"He's got an EEG," a medical student reported excitedly from the monitors.

Albert jumped to his feet and tried to get closer, but the doctors and nurses were crowding around. They didn't want my family to get close until they had thoroughly examined me.

After he was certain I was conscious, Albert ran to get Cheryl. "Tom's opened his eyes, and he's got an EEG," he said. "Come look."

It was almost too much for Cheryl to believe. She had steeled herself against false optimism and had focused so much on enduring through the day despite bad news. She felt relief, but she also realized that she now faced more complex challenges, and she wondered if she or I could cope with the inevitable brain damage. The relief at my recovery and the new challenges pulled her mind in opposite directions as she walked toward the room.

As the doctors crowded around my bed, I motioned to one of them to get my Bible. He picked it up and laid it open on my chest. The passage exposed was Isaiah 61:

"The Spirit of the Lord God is upon me,

Because the LORD has anointed me

To bring good news to the afflicted;

He has sent me to bind up the brokenhearted,

To proclaim liberty to captives,
And freedom to prisoners. . . .

I read those verses and grinned, and the doctor picked it up and read it. He marked the passage and later showed it to Cheryl.

When she entered the room, the doctors and nurses were still crowding around my bed. Cheryl could only get a peep at me from a distance as she tried to prepare herself for dealing with a hopelessly brain-damaged husband.

She walked to the corner of the room and heard the nurses recount what had happened. The news was almost too good to believe, and Cheryl chattered loudly about the difficulties of the previous week and a half.

I heard her talking and thought she was arguing with the nurses. I motioned for a pencil and paper and scrawled a barely legible note: "Keep your big mouth shut and go to church."

One of the nurses carried it to her, and I watched her read it. She turned and looked at me with a puzzled look.

I was pointing at her and gesturing. *What did I do?* she thought *What did I do?* She was shocked. All she had been thinking about for ten days was my welfare, and one of the first things I did after regaining consciousness was reprimand her. It was so unexpected, and she felt so betrayed. It probably hurt her more than anything in her life.

She watched me gesturing angrily at her, and her arms fell to her sides. She began to cry, bowing her head and holding her face with her hands. Her shoulders shook as she wept bitterly and walked slowly out of the room.

I kept pointing and gesturing at her as she left, but I was puzzled. I couldn't understand why she took it so badly. I was trying to say that time is very short. Don't worry about anything except what's important.

However, I wasn't able to say those things. When my mother saw Cheryl crying, she wanted to know why. She was given the note, and she read it.

Incensed, she walked briskly into the room and scolded me. "How dare you write her a note like this after all she's been through?"

I know it's difficult to imagine that something so trivial could upset people who had been through so much. However, the incident served as a safety valve for a lot of pent-up emotion. My mother now knew that I was going to live, and she again could expect only the best from her son. But I was confused by her anger, not realizing that I was causing pain to those who had grieved intensely for me and prayed so diligently for my recovery.

14

A Standing Ovation

After the doctors thoroughly examined me, they let Cheryl and Albert visit by my bed for a few minutes. I still had a tube down my throat and was hooked up to the monitoring equipment, so actual conversation was impossible. I scribbled a few notes, and they talked to me.

The good news was countered, however, by another setback. That night I contracted a fever, and Cheryl and Albert stayed at the hospital. She sponged me to keep the temperature down and asked questions in an effort to determine the degree of brain damage I had suffered.

"Tom, do we live at 220 Laurel Drive?"

I'd shake my head no.

"How old is Heath, Tom? Is he two?"

I'd nod my head yes.

Cheryl was afraid I had regressed ten years or more and would not remember our marriage. But I thought her questions were dumb and felt very irritated. I didn't understand her concern. My temperature was high. I had a tube down my throat, so I couldn't swallow very well. I ached all over. And my wife was asking me the kinds of questions she might ask a retarded person or a child.

What in the world is wrong with her? I thought. *Why can't she leave me alone?*

I finally became so irritated by the tube down my throat that

I tried to pull it out, and a big male nurse, an Indian, was stationed by my bed to prevent me from doing it again.

I could hear the life support equipment hissing and humming, keeping alive several patients in the room. Occasionally, one of the monitoring machines would buzz, indicating a crisis, and I would get frantic. I thought it was one of my machines and that something was wrong with me.

"Tom, honey. It's not you. It's not you," Cheryl would say, and it would take several minutes for me to calm down.

Thursday night, Albert's wife had called from New Jersey and told him the business needed him badly. Cheryl drove him to the airport early Friday morning. She didn't want Albert to leave. He had helped her make it through many crises, and she had grown to care for him deeply during those days. There were no parking places at the airport, she had to let him off at the airline's door, and she was extremely depressed.

The doctors tried to take the tube from my throat that morning, but I went into convulsions, and they had to put it back. It would be another day before it was removed.

Cheryl also was worried about any psychological problems I might have if Albert was gone without explanation. She took a lot of time to explain to me that Albert had to go home but would be back.

During this time a girl walked up to Cheryl with tears in her eyes. She said that she had worked the night I had been in such trouble with pneumonia.

"My mother and father are Christians," she said. "I had left the church and our faith, but I called my mother and father, and her church and her prayer chain prayed for your husband. The doctors wouldn't have given a wooden nickel for his life, and look at him now. It's a miracle." She paused and then said, "Because of this, I've given my life to Jesus."

Saturday morning, Cheryl asked the doctors if I could come into the lounge in a wheelchair for a few minutes. It was the first time she had really looked at me, and I seemed retarded. I had lost a lot of weight. My neck was thin, and my head looked much bigger than before. There was no fat on my face, and my eyes seemed to bulge out of their sockets. My head looked like a naked skull with a thin layer of skin pulled tightly over it.

I looked hideous, but my behavior was even worse. I didn't seem to realize that Cheryl and the doctors had thought I would die or be brain-damaged. I didn't realize how seriously ill I had been. Nor did I realize that they did not know I had been aware of everything that was happening around me during the ten days I had been without brain waves.

In that time I had dreamt about trying to say "supercalifrajalisticexpialadocious" over a public-address system. Now I was awake, and I didn't understand that it had been a dream. I thought Cheryl had been there with me, and I was trying to remember the word as I was helped into the wheelchair and rolled toward the lounge.

"What's the word, Cheryl?" I demanded. "Super— Super— You know. You were always smarter than me, Cheryl. You're always smarter than me. What's the word?"

I couldn't understand why Cheryl did not remember the word, and why she was treating me like such a simpleton. I became extremely upset and swung at ashtrays and lamps, trying to knock them over.

There were a lot of people in the lobby, and I was acting like a child or a retarded person. Everybody seemed to be watching me, and there was pity on their faces. *Poor woman,* they seemed to be thinking. *She's been through ten days of fighting death, and now she has the rest of her life with a retarded husband.*

My mother felt their stares, and her face burned with shame as Cheryl knelt beside the wheelchair and asked me, "Tom, where do you live? Do we live at 220 Laurel Drive?"

That made me even angrier. In slowly measured words I said, "You think I'm stupid."

"How old is Heath? Heath is one, right?" she said, ignoring my statement.

I thought about her question and said, "No, Heath is two."

My answers were correct, but Cheryl *knew* I was brain-damaged. Why else would I act that way? I pushed at things near me and hit at Cheryl with my arm. She didn't realize that I was merely recovering my mental equilibrium. She thought I was hopelessly retarded.

That afternoon the Jorgensons brought Heath to the hospital, and they all decided to go to an ice-skating show. My mother had never been to that kind of show, and Cheryl's mother hadn't gone since Frick and Fratt in the 1930s. Nancy Jorgenson had a friend who worked at the Oakland Coliseum and was able to get front-row seats.

They all had a good time. It was such a change from the death and trauma of the hospital, and they enjoyed watching the ice skaters. Cheryl took instant pictures of Heath and Big Bird. When they returned, she placed them on my bedside table in the hospital room.

Jim Cojanis met them at the hospital, and Cheryl asked him to take Cheryl's mother to our house with Heath. We thought that Heath needed to return home, and our mail had been piling up. Jim took them home, and my mother moved into the motel room with Cheryl.

Meanwhile, the doctors were concerned about my bizarre behavior, and a psychiatrist was called. Cheryl introduced herself to him and said, "It's not a psychiatric problem. All the machines and the intensity of the room are upsetting him. I think he'll be better off in another room. If he could just be in a two-man intensive care unit, I think he would be better."

On Sunday, Cheryl talked with one of the doctors. "Let's move him out of this room," she said. "That's his problem." They took her advice, and I was moved into a two-person room.

That night I became tired of lying in bed, and I wanted to know what had happened to me to cause such fuss. I got out of bed and walked down the hall. I had shown no motor control in my legs, so the doctors assumed that my legs were paralyzed and never dreamed I would try to walk.

I caught everybody by surprise when a nurse shrieked, "He's walking!" She acted as if she had seen a dead man. She had rounded a corner, and there I was, a skinny hulk, clad only in a short hospital gown, shuffling down the hall, carrying my bottle of intravenous fluid. I looked like something out of a Dracula movie.

I didn't get to the nurses' station. Nurses came rushing up with orderlies and interns. "What happened to me?" I mumbled.

"There have been some complications, but you're better now," was the reply.

The next day, Dr. Myer Rosenthal talked to me, and Dr. Hass and a number of doctors examined me. Then Dr. Steve Rosenthal and a woman doctor named Marilee entered the room.

"I know you," I said. "You're my doctors."

They had been off-duty when I had regained consciousness, so I could not have known who they were unless I knew what was happening around me during the days that I had shown a flat EEG.

But Marilee dismissed my recognition of them. "The drugs caused you to have dreams," she said.

I must be confused, I thought, and I didn't talk about my experience in detail for several weeks. In fact, it was more than a month before I told Cheryl everything. We were driving on the expressway to San Jose, and I said, "I wish you'd throw that shawl away. It smells. I hate that shawl. You wore it almost every day I was in the hospital, and I couldn't stand it."

Obviously, I had been through an experience that was not normal, and both Cheryl and I were having a tough time adjusting. As much as a year later, Cheryl would be washing dishes and looking out the window at the Redwoods in the valley near Felton. It was a beautiful view, and her thoughts would wander.

Suddenly she would find herself reliving scenes from the hospital. She would feel she was back there, seeing that cold, still body lying on the cooling table. That experience has happened several times in the last few years, both to Cheryl and to her mother. However, it doesn't happen as often now.

During my last few days in the hospital, I spent a lot of time walking, and I was moved to the orthopedic ward. I could walk upright now instead of bent over like an ape. I had no pain. My back was well, even though Dr. Hass had not performed the delicate surgical procedure for which I had been admitted. I was told I could go home.

On June 2, eighteen days after I had been admitted, Dr. Hass came in and went through his routine. Then Dr. Walker visited for a long time.

"You know, you people go to the right church," Dr. Walker said before he left the room. "I know you do."

Cheryl thanked him for his concern. Then she got the car, parked it by the door, and came to my room for me.

Slowly we walked arm and arm down the corridor. The people in the lounge knew who I was and that I was going home. One by one they stood up and began clapping, and some came up and shook my hand. It was amazing, a standing ovation, acknowledging my God, the One who has power over death.

Even now, I still don't think I fully realize what God has done for me. However, that I am alive is a testimony to what He can do in the life of a self-centered person like me. I can tell you that I am alive today because the God of Abraham, Isaac, and Jacob acts in the lives of sinful persons and responds to the pleas of penitent believers.

Truly, He has given me abundant life.

15

A Place of Service

In the weeks that followed my hospitalization, I learned that the heavy doses of thiopental sodium and the "cooling" bed procedures were in experimental stages and used only in extreme cases. Dr. Myer Rosenthal explained the process in the February 1978 issue of the prestigious *Western Journal of Medicine.* In an article there, he described four patients at Stanford who had been without blood to the brain more than "seven to ten minutes." I was one of the four, and each of us underwent this "super heroic" treatment. Two of us recovered without brain damage.

One of the Stanford doctors told Grant Hardin, a reporter for the San Jose *Mercury News,* that I was fortunate. "There is no question but that he suffered a severe insult to the brain," the doctor is reported to have said.

Hardin reports that doctors at Stanford were not willing to say that I was ever medically dead. Their uncertainty was the result of not being able to define death precisely. Does death arrive when a person's heart stops or when all brain activity ceases? Is it both? Or is it something else altogether? Previously, death had been defined as a flat EEG, no brain waves. I had a flat EEG, but it was the result of chemical inducement. Because the doctors did not have time to record my EEG before beginning "super heroic" treatment, they were unwilling to say I was dead. However, they admit that my recovery was extremely unusual. One Palo Alto anesthesiologist called it "miraculous."

Hardin reports that the doctors distinguish between my experience and that of Karen Ann Quinlan, a young woman who remained in a comatose state even after being disconnected from an artificial life support system. *Coma* is a term used to describe a state of unconsciousness in which there usually is some brain function. My brain was not functioning, according to the monitoring machines.

As I tried to comprehend that experience, I became convinced that I did not die. I believe that God gave the doctors special wisdom and kept life in me through those ten days. And I know that He answered my earnest prayers as I lingered between life and death.

That experience helped me to understand that a person's view of death is based on his concept of God. If He is not a just God, if He does not require a penalty for sin, if the death of His son, Jesus, does not mean anything, then God does not distinguish between death for those who believe in Him and death for those who do not.

In recent years, the writings and lectures of Raymond A. Moody, Jr., and Elizabeth Kübler-Ross, two prominent doctors, have caused many people to believe that life after death is happy. They have accepted God's justice. In fact, the life-after-death experiences that Kübler-Ross and Moody have described may have encouraged many people to lose their fear of death. That is enhanced by their failure to call attention to the pain and suffering involved in death. As a result, people who wish a better life feel encouraged to commit suicide. That is clearly dangerous, and it's not God's way.

Writing to the Corinthian church, the apostle Paul made it very clear that death was to be feared if it were to be faced without faith in the resurrected Christ. In other words, life after death may not be happy, and only through Christ is there victory over the power of death.

The Lord offers us the gift of life and commands us to be His representatives on earth. It's an insult to the Lord to want to voluntarily leave this earth.

Obviously, I disagree with Moody and Kübler-Ross because the Bible does, but I also differ with them by experience. Moody describes a typical near-death experience in which the victim encountered spirits of dead relatives and friends who talked with him nonverbally. He writes about floating, about an extremely bright light that spoke to the person, about an indescribable love. Similarly, Kübler-Ross talks about ''out of body'' experiences in which she has met ''spirit guides'' who reported to her on life after death.

Similarly, after the trauma on the operating table, something touched me, and I felt engulfed in complete warmness, surrounded by a comforting brightness, unlike the brightness from the sun or anything equivalent here on earth. It's difficult to describe those moments, but I did feel peace—that every problem, every care had been lifted from my shoulders. However, I did not pass through a tunnel, and I did not bump into dead relatives or friends. My experience also differed in that I could see my family and friends. I knew they were around me, that they were suffering, and I wanted to reach out and comfort them in their pain. I grieved for them in their bereavement. Moreover, I experienced judgment, deep anguish, and a need for earnest repentance. I saw everything wrong that I had ever done in a panoramic view, all at once. It was like a movie shown on all sides of the theater at once, and I could see it all. I knew that I needed forgiveness, that I had not served the Lord. And I begged for mercy.

It is this experience of judgment that has interested Christians. Within days of my release from the hospital, I was invited to give my testimony in churches throughout the area. People called and wrote me for counsel. In the ensuing three years, I have spoken to more than two hundred churches and organizations, given lectures, and conducted seminars on faith and commitment and workshops on counseling. I have appeared on radio and television programs and preached many sermons on faith and life and death.

Through this exposure, the outreach ministries of Cliffwood Heights Neighborhood Church have expanded phenomenally. Before the hospital incident, my counseling had been limited, for the most part, to our church. Now it has grown in numbers and in the areas of ministry. I began to counsel in nursing homes, do a lot of marital counseling, visit terminally ill in hospitals, and work with juvenile offenders through youth court. Clearly, ten days with a flat EEG drew headlines that gave the counseling ministry many open doors.

One place I visited often was a Christian nursing home in Felton. Unfortunately, there were conflicts among the residents, and many of them didn't trust each other. I emphasized that they still had responsibilities to contribute to the community. I didn't talk to them as though they were old people, and over time several became Christians.

One afternoon, Alma, a woman in her late eighties, called me. "My husband doesn't love me anymore," she said.

I could hardly believe my ears. Here was a woman who could hardly walk and whose husband had been bedridden with Hodgkin's disease for many years, and she was concerned about romance.

"He hasn't kissed me for five years because he thinks I'm sleeping with another man, and he won't talk decently to me," she added.

She was lonely. Her husband of many years was treating her badly. I promised her I would visit her husband that afternoon.

"My name is Tom Scarinci," I said when I walked into the room, and John looked away. "I thought I'd stop in."

"Who sent you?"

"Nobody really."

"I bet my wife put you up to this."

"No. I talked to your wife briefly, and she told me how

ornery you are, but I didn't believe her. Now that I've seen you, I realize how obnoxious you are.''

''What'd she tell you?''

''Nothing much. Just that you're a hard individual.''

He was a proud German man whose paralysis had even affected his facial muscles, and he could not move his head. He told me to get out and never come back.

''Listen,'' I said. ''It's nobody's fault that you're lying in this bed right now. There's nothing you can do about it. God's got you here.''

It was as though I had thrown ice water in his face. Despite his paralysis, his eyes showed amazement. He wasn't used to someone talking back to him in the way he talked to them.

''I can understand how you might feel sorry for yourself,'' I said. ''I know it must make you feel inadequate, but you can't change your physical condition. You can do something about your wife's situation. She has a burden that you have made heavier by your attitude. She's devoted her life to you. In spite of your rudeness, she's come to see you several times a day and sat by your bed for hours.''

My words were sinking in. He didn't like what I said, but he knew I was describing his situation, and he respected the fact that I was straightforward and didn't feel sorry for him.

''Yet, you don't trust your wife. You've shut her out,'' I said.

''Oh, that's nonsense.''

''No. It's something you better face because you're getting ready to die. You can make your death a beautiful thing or horrible.''

I then told him about my life, and he thought it was just a lot of hogwash because of his illness.

''Listen,'' I told him. ''You've been a broken down man for years, not able to function. Yet you let your filthy mind wander and you think suspiciously about a woman who served you and trusted you. Has your wife ever been unfaithful to you?''

"No. She was a good woman," he admitted. He knew she was not an immoral person, but he pitied himself and the inadequacy of his situation. He had traveled throughout the world in his business, and he had been aggressive and extremely successful. He hated failure and weakness. He couldn't accept failure in himself, and he couldn't blame his wife because he had Hodgkin's disease, but he could try to make her feel guilty for his misery.

"Well, when I'd be away for months at a time, I couldn't be expected to be perfect," he said, and he bragged about his extramarital affairs.

"How brazen can you be?" I said. "You live a life of sin. Then, when you're an invalid, you accuse your wife of the very things you did. It's your filthy mind. You better shape up. God can forgive you, but you've got to want to be forgiven."

He didn't say anything.

I reached for my wallet and pulled it out; "If you need me, here's my card," I said, handing it to him.

I left the hospital at about 7:30 P.M. and thought about the old man throughout the evening. Before going to bed, Cheryl and I spent several minutes in prayer, mentioning John, among others. As we prayed the phone rang. It was John, and his words were interspersed with deep sobs.

He had been so convicted that he had awakened the person in the bed next to him to call my telephone number and hold the phone next to his ear.

"Please pray for me, pastor," he said. "I'm afraid."

After he hung up, I drove to the home and we talked and prayed together, and he accepted the Lord into his life.

The next afternoon, his wife called and asked me to come see her at her house in Felton.

She was crying when I arrived.

"I'm so happy," she said. "My husband took me by the hand this morning, and we talked for a long time. He told me he accepted Jesus."

That night I visited him in the nursing home, and we prayed. When we were finished, he whispered for me to hold him. I put my arms around him, put my face next to his face, and kissed him. "I love you," he said, and closed his eyes. A few minutes later he was dead.

John and Alma are an unusual example, but their case shows how the terminally ill affected me. They helped to destroy my deep-seated stereotypes about older people not being interested in romance. And by John's response to the gospel, I had concrete evidence of God's forgiveness, and the changes it produces in lives.

Jeff is another case. He was a Christian who had lived an active church life, even serving as head deacon. He was dying of cancer and in intense pain. When we prayed together, he would pray for God to take him home. He couldn't bear the pain.

I listened to him complain for several sessions. He had legitimate complaints. His pain was so intense that he could hardly stand to have anyone touching the bed.

"Jeff," I said, "I know you are in great pain, but your self-pity is not what Jesus expects from you."

"What do you mean?" he asked.

"You're in a place of ministry, a community of nonbelievers. Jesus expects you to use this opportunity to witness for Him."

I had his attention. In fact, I believe he was so surprised by my comments that he had forgotten his pain.

"Jesus brings life and healing. You don't have a right to pray to God to take away your life."

"I know," Jeff said. "I've forgotten about all the others."

"That's right," I said. "No matter how bad the situation, when Jesus is in your life, He offers encouragement, compassion, and love for God."

Jeff responded to my encouragement. He prayed to the Lord for grace to minister to others, and during his last few days he was an example of how God's grace can change every difficult situation.

Many terminally ill people know they're dying. However, the family often doesn't know because the doctors don't want to tell them their efforts have not been successful. As a result, I often tell the family the news. I explain to them that the patient knows and wants to talk about it. He wants to know who is going to take care of various details, and he wants to encourage those whom he is leaving behind. Similarly, Jeff ministered to his relatives. He comforted them before his death.

The secular person often attempts to ease the pain of death by avoiding its reality. Death is not meant to be beautiful for the unsaved (Rom. 6:23). It is caused by sin and is excruciatingly painful when faced without God.

Being a counselor to dying people has made me aware of the uniqueness of each individual. Repeatedly I have been reminded of my limited lifespan and its place in the multitude that forms the Kingdom of God. Such realizations have helped me to be a better counselor to those who are dying. They have given me new purpose in life. The problems that the Lord has sent me were enabling me to help others. Obviously, I had known that life was not easy, that it included starvation, immorality, murder, and other intense suffering. But that knowledge had always depressed me. Now I was realizing that problems can be converted into vehicles of service.

As the months passed, the public schools, the California Youth Authority, the Juvenile Hall, and ministers in the area were referring people to me.

One evening, Don and Betty came to see me. They lived in San Jose. They were strong, committed Christians. Don was a deacon in the church, and Betty had been active in church all her life. They had been married about five years and had two daughters, three and five years of age. But for nearly a year, Betty had been having blackouts, a nervous stomach, and diarrhea. For months they had tried to find out what was causing the blackouts. Doctor after doctor examined her, but nobody could find any physical problem. It was suggested that she had a psychosomatic problem and that a psychiatrist might be able to unlock the cause. Betty rejected that. She knew her problem was physical, yet she could find no relief. She finally agreed to see a Christian counselor, and her minister referred her to me.

As they described her problem, they were extremely protective of one another, and we didn't make much progress during the first few visits.

During the first session, we talked for about ten minutes, and then I led in prayer. I asked the Lord for sensitivity and for Him to open me up to Betty's suffering. I wanted to be vulnerable to her hurt.

Then I explained to Betty that she had seen some of the best doctors in the country, and that I was merely an associate minister of a small church. It was not what I would do that would help her, but what Jesus Christ could do through me and her working together. I explained that only as she trusted completely in Him would I be able to help her.

I quickly learned that the blackouts came four or five times a day, lasting anywhere from one minute to three, and that when they came Betty would feel as though she were being crushed and suffocated.

Her blackouts "happened all the time," Betty explained.

I thought for a moment and then said, "Do they occur when you're out having a good time?"

"No," Don said.

"Have you taken any trips or done things together that were special fun?"

"Yeah. We went to Disneyland for a couple of weeks."

"Has it ever happened during those trips?"

"No," he said.

"But it happened last night after we went out to eat," Betty said.

"When?" I asked.

"When we came home."

"Look, if it is basically a physical problem, isn't it unusual that you've never blacked out when you were doing something you enjoyed?" I asked.

Betty was silent, and I paused.

"Betty, I believe it is psychosomatic," I said, and she looked horror-stricken. "That doesn't mean it's not real," I added quickly. "A psychosomatic illness is just as real as a physical illness, and you should not feel guilty about it."

In later interviews, I probed more deeply and learned about Don's and Betty's problems.

In those sessions they were less tolerant of each other, each blaming the other for many of the problems. Gradually, I moved toward the heart of the problem and began meeting with them in separate sessions.

Then Betty began to tell the whole story.

She had volunteered before she was married to do missionary work in Europe for a summer. During her duty, she was taken to a van and raped by seven men who were associated with the mission.

She had suppressed the incident, but her subconscious mind kept trying to find a way to release the guilt and shame. She started to experience blackouts. They increased as the years passed until her very marriage was in jeopardy.

As we began to get closer to the problem during the counseling sessions, her guilty feelings became more evident. On at least two occasions she attempted suicide. She would experience periods of hysteria in which she would relive the rape scene, calling on God not to let them rape her.

The details are too gruesome to describe in detail, and that's why she had tried to forget the incident, to drive it from her experience; and blackouts resulted. She desperately wanted to keep it from her husband. Then we brought the incident into the open in counseling sessions. Finally, she understood that she had to tell her husband about the incident. It was painful, but now Don knows about everything, and Betty and he are enjoying a warm, happy marriage without blackouts.

I also make regular rounds to the hospitals. One sunny afternoon, I heard there was a bad case in the emergency room, and I thought I would try to help.

A short, heavyset woman with stringy hair and bloodshot eyes was standing near one of the rooms in intensive care. She looked at me bleary-eyed and brought a styrofoam cup shakily to her lips.

I introduced myself, and she explained that her boyfriend had been drinking when he drove his automobile into a tree. Investigators estimated his speed at impact at ninety miles per hour.

I walked into the room and saw a man no older than thirty-five. His skull was fractured, and his head was twice its normal size. His eyes seemed to bulge out, and his face was so discolored that it looked black. His torn mouth was stitched, and a respirator had been inserted. His appearance was nauseating.

I walked up to his bedside, took him by the hand, and prayed softly but audibly that he might hear the gospel if there was life in him.

Then I went out into the hall. By now several relatives had arrived, and they were making a lot of noise. Many of them were hung over, and others had alcohol on their breath. As we talked, the man's girlfriend nearly collapsed with grief. I asked the family to meet at seven o'clock the next evening at Cliffwood Heights Neighborhood Church. They thought it was a routine prefuneral arrangement.

I could tell the family had great psychological and spiritual needs. Later I learned that it was a family with a great deal of hostility. None of them seemed to be able to get along, and many of them had never been in a church.

Just before seven, they started arriving at the church. They walked quietly down the aisle to sit in the few pews near the front. Some of them were drunk.

I spoke a few words about life and death and said that Jesus offers a quality of life that cannot be found in alcohol. Then we prayed for the patient. It was not a long prayer sesson, but the peace and quiet of our sanctuary brought a hush to those people, and they sat extremely still. After the service, the hospital called the church to tell us the man had died.

But in his death, his godless relatives had the opportunity to hear the gospel. And several later made commitments to Christ.

Often I don't learn about people until it's too late. Early one morning, a woman telephoned my office from Watsonville.

"Are you Rev. Scarinci?" she asked.

"Yes."

"You're the man in Stanford Hospital with no brain waves for ten days?"

"Right."

"I need your help. My best friend has just died and is in the morgue at the hospital. Would you pray for him?"

She wanted me to go to the morgue, lay hands on him, and pray for him. She thought there was magic in my hands, that I had a special contact with God.

"I'm sorry," I said. "I can't bring people from the dead. I can't even pray for them in that situation. But I can pray for you that you will have peace."

She never came to see me, but I recalled how lonely I had felt in the hospital, and how I had wanted someone to tell me he cared.

I've tried to implement that in my counseling. I want people who hurt to know that I care and that because of Jesus I love them.

When a person walks into my office, I want him to know that I love him unconditionally.

"No matter what happens," I tell everyone, "I love you, and you can't change my mind."

People have spit at me, thrown plants and chairs, and broken windows, but they soon realize they can't make me hate them.

If I can get a person to understand that he is worth something, he can make progress. I try to do that by being an agent of God's love.

I also try to be honest with those who come to me for counseling. Jesus didn't compromise. He described reality.

As a counseling session develops, I listen. Sometimes I will listen almost the entire time. If I don't think the person is being honest with me, I may say, "I've been listening to you, watching your eyes, watching you move. And you're communicating a lot more than what you're putting in words."

That statement surprises most people.

"Three-fourths of what you've said isn't real," I go on. "So we're not going to get to the problem. I have no right to play with your life. It's my job to be direct with you, and that's why I want you to know that you're doing what the typical person does. You're playing games."

That usually makes a person feel angry and guilty. Some may want to withdraw. But I usually continue.

"You are going to open up this pain that's inside of you, or you will be burdened for a long time."

Usually people respond. Sometimes I need to reinforce what I've said by telling them that I'm a representative of the Lord. When they lie to me, they're lying to the Lord.

People who come to me for counseling normally don't have to see me longer than three weeks. Most of the people with whom I work believe they have spiritual problems. I deal with that honestly. I focus on the fact that a person can't forgive himself until he asks God for forgiveness. When he asks, God forgives. If I don't accept that forgiveness and forgive myself, I'm sinning. Because I deal with the spiritual in all my counseling sessions, I assume that my first responsibility is to help the person accept Jesus into his or her life. Once there is a commitment to the Lord, the Holy Spirit is at work, helping the counselor.

If a person does not accept Christ, I do not stop seeing him until he does. I continue to love and show that he is making no commitment to correct the problems. I support him, and often such people make progress.

I also work with the courts in the Santa Cruz area, visiting prisons and working with juveniles. I'll work with the judge and set up a counseling program for young people who otherwise would go to the detention center. I make them follow a disciplined counseling program, meeting with me every week. The juveniles know that if they miss one session with me, the probation is finished, and they will have to go to the detention center.

Through hundreds of cases, I have found that those prisoners and juveniles who are converted have a much greater chance of not returning to prison.

Most prisoners have been responsive. I have worked with drug addicts, murderers, armed robbers, burglars, child molesters, rapists, and rape victims. About one-fourth of them have become Christians, and I don't know of one convert who has returned to jail.

Sometimes counseling prisoners is frightening. I was going to see prisoners on Sundays in the Santa Cruz County Correction Facility.

I was standing in the middle of the big lockup room one Sunday, talking to a prisoner that I had known for some time.

A big black man came up behind me as we talked and jerked my Bible, which I had tucked under my arm.

"Hey, what is this? Are you a preacher?" he asked in a scoffing manner.

"Wait a minute, brother," I said without turning around. "I'm talking with this man. I'll be with you in a minute."

But he continued to chatter and ridicule me. His antics were stirring the fifteen to twenty other prisoners, and I became concerned that the situation might get out of hand.

I whirled around, looked up into his face, and pointed my finger at him.

"You move before you find out how powerful this Bible is," I ordered. But he didn't move.

I thrust my finger in his chest. "Move," I yelled, and he did.

Then I returned to my earlier conversation, explaining to that prisoner that he had a responsibility to minister to his fellow prisoners. I explained that even though he was in jail, no one could lock up his soul, and often prisoners were looking for freedom. He could show them how to get it.

Meanwhile, the big black fellow was trying to listen. When we finished he called to me, "Hey, buddy, come here."

I walked over to him.

"Is that really true?"

"Yes," I said, and we talked for several minutes. At the end of our conversation, he accepted the Lord.

Later he asked me about that incident. "Did that book keep you from being afraid of me?" he said.

"No, I was scared, but I trust in this book," I said. "It helps me do things I don't otherwise have guts to do."

I've found that many churches in the area will work with prisoners, but they're not too eager to accept them in their congregations once they're released. That has made our ministry difficult.

Nonetheless, lay people are working with us. During the fall of 1979, we began a Bible-oriented training program at Cliffwood Heights Neighborhood Church to develop paraprofessionals in the counseling ministry. Through a carefully designed curriculum, we have been able to help them identify problems, develop techniques for counseling in times of temporary stress, and gain expertise in distinguishing whether more professional help is needed.

We repeatedly remind those in the program that the main objective is discipleship. We want them to learn how to disciple people whom they identify as needing counsel.

Nine persons were graduated from our first class during the spring of 1980. They were from four or five churches in the area, and they attended Saturday classes for six months.

After covering basic biblical principles, we brought in persons who discussed their situation. Often they were people who had come to me for counseling.

I also am staff counselor at Monte Vista Christian School, an interdenominational, coeducational school on a ninety-acre campus in Watsonville. There are residential and day-student programs for the seventh through twelfth grades. Nearly four hundred students enroll at Monte Vista from around the world.

I'm the campus pastor and director of spiritual counseling. I act as a liaison between students and faculty, and I'm involved in the spiritual development of the students.

These and many other opportunities have developed as I have grown in the faith. Today I am a living example of what God can do despite human weaknesses. He offers life, and He requires us to use our lives to save others.

I am grateful that He had mercy on me and gave me these opportunities to serve Him.

Appendix: Medical Summary by Joost Sluis, M.D.

On April 4, 1979, I first had an opportunity to meet Thomas Scarinci as a patient who had been involved in an auto accident. He was referred to me as an orthopedic surgeon because of an injury to the right wrist, which had been caught in the steering wheel of his car. The injury was relatively minor, and was treated easily without subsequent complications.

His main concern was a flare-up of low back pain with radiation to both legs. He was again acutely uncomfortable, but had been well since his Stanford admission. The history in regard to this problem is partially obtained from the Stanford records of March and May 1977, and the information he was able to provide. It essentially summarizes rather briefly his prolonged and complicated medical history in this regard. He first noted pain in the low back in 1972. In addition, at the time of onset he had neck complaints and an operation had been performed consisting of a "fusion" of two of the vertebrae in the lower neck. He had been free of symptoms subsequently and had a happy result.

However, his back pain had persisted since 1972. He had burning pain in the low back and legs with radiation more to the right leg than the left. Normal sensations occurred in his right foot, and he complained of toe numbness. There had been no fractures at this location, but he had had several injuries in 1974 and 1976 to the low back, exacerbating his complaints. Usually his pains were intensified when standing and sitting and improved with bed rest, heat, and so on. He had no other complications implicating damage to the nerves of his lower body.

Approximately ten diagnostic studies had been performed through the years. In May 1977 he underwent an operative procedure at Stanford University for the low back complaints, and during this procedure he had a stoppage of the heart. This will be discussed in more detail below. He had had an adverse reaction to an injection of dye for a study of arteries previously, but the possibility of its being related to the cardiac arrest is unknown.

On my physical examination in April 1979, he had considerable tenderness over the lower back. There was a well-healed scar which extended to the left in a J-shaped fashion. On thumping his back, there was an increase in the complaints of pain. Initially it was not possible to put his hip through a range of motion because of the marked pain radiating from the back. He had an area of diminished or altered sensation in much of the right lower extremity that was explainable on the basis of involvement of two nerves from his spine. He also had weakness on coming up on tiptoes, with pain and disability of the type sometimes known as dystrophy. Occasional marked spasms would occur in some muscle groups of his leg, initially relieved by trying to relax the muscle.

The one additional finding was that he had apparently had some bleeding in the globe of his eye, but this quickly cleared after an ophthalmologic consultation and in a matter of only a few days.

I refer to the Stanford orthopedic surgeon in regard to the findings of his X rays. He reported that he had an abnormal joint between two of the lower back vertebrae and that one had slipped forward of the other. The purpose of the operation in May 1977 had been to make these two vertebrae solid so that the motion at the painful site would be eliminated and relieve him of symptoms.

An additional finding on general and physical examination

was a small lump in the lower abdomen which has been observed for some time and has not enlarged. Only observation at this time is indicated to rule out any possible uncontrolled growth of this lump and its possible biopsy and removal at some future time. Today, Tom occasionally requires intramuscular medication for relief of his pain, and this he has been able to limit and control quite adequately under my close supervision.

Tom's Illness May 16 to June 2, 1977

Tom was admitted to Stanford University Hospital on May 16, 1977, for a "laminectomy and fusion." An orthopedic surgeon performed these procedures, which consist of exploring the nerves in the lower back that may be affected in the symptoms and pain of which he complained and uniting by bone the two vertebrae that were involved, causing the pain from the joint between the two.

The day of operation was May 16, 1977, and Tom was given medication before surgery to prepare him for a spinal anesthetic.

3:10 P.M.   Spinal anesthesia was instituted using Pontocaine 12 mg. in 10 cc of distilled water. The patient was awake and placed in the prone position. His hips and knees, therefore, were flexed, and his back was pointing upward with his head down on the operating table. Tom had been told to raise his head if he wanted sedation.

3:27 P.M.   Surgery was begun on his lower back through J-shaped incision.

3:42 P.M.   The patient raised his head, and he was given more sedative, and settled down again. About 45 seconds after the sedative, Tom became bluish in color. His pulse at that moment was not detectable. The electrical waves from his heart (EKG) looked relatively normal. The anesthesiologist felt that he had had a severe pressure drop and noted that he stopped breathing. Pure oxygen was given by mask, and a medication to attempt to raise his blood pressure. He momentarily became more pink but then became bluish again (cyanotic). His heart rate began to slow on the EKG.

3:45 P.M. Patient was turned on a table onto his back, and cardiopulmonary resuscitation (CPR), in an attempt to start his heart and respiration again, was started. By this time, there was no electrical activity from his heart, and the EKG was flat. The OR (Operating Room) team continued compression of the heart at regular intervals, color again improved, but no electrical heart activity was observed. His color again became worse and his pupils enlarged, a sign of inadequate oxygen to the brain, ischemia. Repeated injections into his heart were performed to stimulate it, but the heart went into a grossly irregular rhythm (ventricular fibrillation).

3:59 P.M. Effective heart action was established for the first time since the start of CPR (14 minutes before). At that time, one gram, a very large dose, of sodium pentothal was given slowly intravenously at the direction of the physician who supervised his care during the remainder of his hospitalization. The Pentothal produced again stoppage of his breathing and a marked fall in his blood pressure. After an hour, Tom was returned to the Intensive Care Unit after the wound was closed in a rapid fashion. The operation was never completed.

The anesthesiologist at that time felt that it was likely that air had traveled to his heart from some of the veins in the back. This indeed is a very rare complication of this type of surgery. He postulated that this had occurred because he temporarily improved on initial CPR, and there was subsequent extreme difficulty in resuscitating a relatively young man. The doctor on more recent conversation felt that it was probably more likely that the spinal anesthestic had traveled in an untoward way, and that this produced the cardiac and respiratory arrest.

During the CPR, electrical stimulation of the heart (defibrillation) was used at 6, 11, and 14 minutes after the CPR was started. Forty-one minutes into the arrest, he was given Decadron 8 mg. to help protect the brain. The sodium pentothal was given for the same reason beginning slowly at 14 minutes, as discussed in more detail below. Many other medications were also given throughout the resuscitation, and wound closure was done at about an hour after the arrest. The criterion for the termination of dose of sodium pentothal was to achieve a blood level between 40 and 90 micrograms per milliliter and no electrical brain waves (isoelectric electroencephalogram) for 72 hours. It should be noted that the electroencephalogram was not monitored during the initial period of the arrest, but only after the sodium pentothal was started. The purpose of this treatment was to give the brain use of glucose (metabolic rate) at 30 to 50 percent of normal so that while brain swelling is maximal between 36 to 72 hours, the amount of cell damage will be minimized. Dose of Pentothal is a high one, and it did as expected produce cardiac depression. Medications to maintain an affective average blood pressure were given throughout this period of time. It was also postulated that he might have had an adverse reaction to the prepping solution for his skin that was used. This apparently was subsequently fairly well ruled out.

The patient remained comatose, and his body temperature was reduced by cooling to about 86 degrees fahrenheit (30 to 32 degrees Centigrade). This again was done to help protect the brain and reduce its nutrient requirements, including oxygen. The blood values of various chemicals and normal constituents were carefully monitored throughout his postoperative course. A review of his medical chart revealed close and expert medical management throughout his course.

The cortisone-like compound Decadron and the Pentothal were discontinued on the third postarrest day. On that day he also developed an acute respiratory syndrome characterized by an elevation in temperature and some deterioration in his condition. Tom's wife was advised that he remained in critical condition. The cause for this complication remains unknown, though it is not uncommonly observed in this kind of surgical complication. The appearance of the chest X ray confirmed the presence of this problem; listening to his lungs also revealed abnormal sounds. The fourth day was a day of continued deterioration, but on the fifth day, there was general improvement, though he remained comatose.

On the seventh day, he was coughing because of the tube that remained in his throat, and his pupils began to react. Ventilation of his lungs improved. He began to respond to deep painful stimuli.

On about the tenth postoperative day, the patient was doing well and was for the first time oriented and alert. The throat tube in the windpipe was removed on the twelfth postoperative day. At that time, he was doing well, and a full recovery was anticipated. He was begun on slow increased activity such as early walking. Initially, he was confused and rather agitated and given medication to control his excited behavior. This quickly cleared and is commonly seen in patients surrounded by people twenty-four hours a day and who have many tubes inserted into their body in the Intensive Care Unit. Furthermore, Tom realized by this time that the surgery had not been performed and that he may have future bouts of back pain. He continued to improve and was subsequently discharged from the hospital.

Discussion

Thomas Scarinci's clinical course at Stanford University was one of the cases out of four reported in the *Western Journal of Medicine*.[1] He and one other patient in that series recovered without any neurologic damage. The article mentions that "recent studies suggest that barbiturates (such as pentothal) may have a protective effect following both focal and global ischemia." The word *ischemia* refers to inadequate blood supply to the brain, and the word *global* to the fact that it affects the entire brain. The latter is seen in cases of cardiac arrest such as Tom

1. Rosenthal, Myer H. and Larson, C. Phillip, "Protection of the Brain from Progressive Ischemia," *Western Journal of Medicine* 128 (1978):145.

experienced. Tom's period of estimated global cerebral ischemia was in excess of 7 to 10 minutes, according to both Dr. Rosenthal and his anesthesiologist. The usual maximum for severe brain damage to occur, because of severe lack of blood supply to the brain, is 5 minutes. Severe brain damage commonly occurs after as little as two minutes of ischemia. Dr. Rosenthal, in Tom's and my presence, recently said, "The fact that you [Tom] recovered neurologically intact is awesome." He then added humorously, addressing Tom, "If you ascribe your recovery to God, be sure to spell the name right: 'R-o-s-e-n. . . .' "

The article in the *Western Journal of Medicine* concludes as follows: "A prospective randomized study now is necessary to prove the value of this regimen. The dismal neurologic results following cardiac arrests attest to the need for developing improved diagnostic, therapeutic and monitoring techniques in the management of cerebral ischemia."

Tom Scarinci received highly competent and up-to-date medical care. From a review of the available literature, it is very likely that his treatment with barbiturates (pentothal) after his cardiac arrest helped to improve the degree of brain damage he might otherwise have sustained. In a report in 1978, this is confirmed in the conclusion as follows: "By complete neurological recoveries after 5 to 22 minutes of arrest, several of our 14 case reports strongly suggest a brain damage ameliorating effect of barbiturate therapy. Proof of such an effect requires prospective (randomized) multi-institutional clinical studies which are now being initiated." Because, however, of the effect of circulatory depression by barbiturates, the report does not now recommend its use routinely. The report adds, "However, sedative or light anesthetic doses of a barbiturate, combined with relaxant for immobilization and facilitation of controlled hyperventilation, seems justified for routine clinical care, particularly for post-CPR complications, during the crucial first few days following the insult."[2]

2. Breivik, Harold, M.D., et al., "Clinical Feasibility Trials of Barbiturate Therapy after Cardiac Arrest," *Critical Medicine* 6 (1978):228-44.